Low-Code/No-Code Application Development

James Relington

DEDICATION

To those who seek knowledge, inspiration, and new perspectives—
may this book be a companion on your journey, a spark for curiosity,
and a reminder that every page turned is a step toward discovery.

AKNOWLEDGEMENTS

I would like to express my deepest gratitude to everyone who contributed to the creation of this book. To my colleagues and mentors, your insights and expertise have been invaluable. A special thank you to my family and friends for their unwavering support and encouragement throughout this journey.

Introduction to Low-Code/No-Code Development

The world of software development has evolved drastically in recent years, driven by the rapid pace of technological advancement and the increasing demand for faster, more efficient solutions. Traditional software development methods, often relying on complex coding and programming expertise, are now being complemented – and in some cases, replaced – by low-code and no-code development platforms. These platforms have emerged as powerful tools that enable individuals with little to no technical background to create, design, and deploy applications. The rise of low-code and no-code development represents a fundamental shift in how software is created, opening the door to a broader range of people, including business users, to actively participate in the development process.

At the heart of low-code and no-code development is the idea of simplifying the application-building process. Low-code platforms provide a visual interface that allows users to design applications through drag-and-drop elements, minimal coding, and pre-built templates. These platforms often require some basic understanding of coding, but the complexity is significantly reduced, making it more accessible to non-developers. No-code platforms take this concept even further by eliminating the need for any coding at all. Instead, users can create full-fledged applications using visual tools, workflows, and configuration settings. This democratization of development empowers individuals in various industries to bring their ideas to life without the need to rely on specialized developers.

Low-code and no-code platforms offer several advantages over traditional development methods. One of the most significant benefits is speed. Developing an application with traditional coding can be time-consuming and complex, often requiring multiple stages of design, coding, testing, and deployment. In contrast, low-code and no-code platforms significantly reduce the development cycle by allowing users to create applications much more quickly. With pre-built templates, reusable components, and intuitive interfaces, users can assemble applications in a fraction of the time it would take with traditional coding. This accelerated development process is particularly beneficial for businesses looking to quickly respond to market demands, adjust to changing conditions, or launch new products and services.

Another advantage of low-code and no-code development is the cost savings it offers. In traditional development models, businesses often need to hire skilled software developers, project managers, and other IT professionals to build and maintain applications. This can be expensive, especially for small and medium-sized businesses that may not have the budget for extensive development teams. Low-code and no-code platforms reduce this need by enabling non-technical users to create and manage applications themselves. As a result, businesses can save money on development costs, as well as reduce the time spent on hiring and training developers.

The accessibility of low-code and no-code platforms also fosters innovation. By removing the barrier of coding expertise, more people can experiment with and develop new ideas, leading to a wider variety of solutions and products. Business users, for example, can quickly build applications tailored to their specific needs, which may have been previously overlooked by traditional development teams. The ability to prototype and test new ideas rapidly encourages experimentation, ultimately fostering a more agile and innovative approach to application development.

Despite their advantages, low-code and no-code platforms are not without challenges. While they make it easier to create applications, they may not be suitable for every project. Complex applications that require intricate logic, custom integrations, or high performance may still necessitate traditional development methods. Additionally, there may be limitations in terms of customization and flexibility when using low-code or no-code platforms. Some platforms may not allow for the same level of fine-tuning or optimization as traditional coding environments. As a result, developers may face trade-offs between the ease of use provided by low-code/no-code platforms and the need for highly customized or feature-rich applications.

Moreover, as businesses increasingly rely on low-code and no-code solutions, they must consider the long-term sustainability and scalability of their applications. While these platforms are excellent for creating prototypes or simple apps, scaling them for enterprise-level use can be a challenge. As an organization grows, its applications may require more advanced features, better performance, or more robust integrations with other systems. In such cases, businesses may need to transition from low-code or no-code solutions to fully coded applications. This shift may require a more substantial investment in skilled developers and IT infrastructure.

Security is another important consideration in the adoption of low-code and no-code platforms. As with any software, applications built using these platforms must be secure to protect sensitive data and ensure compliance with industry regulations. While many low-code and no-code platforms come with built-in security features, users must be aware of potential vulnerabilities and ensure that they implement best practices for data protection. Organizations must also assess whether the platforms they choose meet the necessary compliance standards for their industry.

Despite these challenges, the low-code and no-code movement continues to grow, driven by the increasing demand for faster development cycles, greater efficiency, and the need to address skill gaps in the workforce. Low-code and no-code platforms are transforming the way organizations think about application development, allowing both technical and non-technical users to collaborate on projects and contribute to the creation of innovative solutions. As these platforms mature and evolve, it is likely that they will become even more powerful and capable, further bridging the gap between business needs and development capabilities.

The future of low-code and no-code development looks promising. With the rise of artificial intelligence, machine learning, and other advanced technologies, these platforms are poised to become even more intelligent and intuitive, enabling users to build more sophisticated applications with even less effort. As businesses continue to embrace digital transformation and the demand for rapid innovation grows, low-code and no-code platforms will play an increasingly vital role in shaping the future of software development. For many organizations, these platforms represent an opportunity to democratize development, reduce costs, speed up time to market, and foster a culture of innovation. By empowering individuals at all levels to participate in the development process, low-code and no-code platforms are helping to redefine what it means to build software in the modern world.

Understanding the Need for Low-Code/No-Code Platforms

The rapid pace of technological change in recent years has led to significant shifts in the way businesses and organizations operate. One of the most notable trends is the increasing reliance on software applications to drive business processes, improve efficiency, and enhance customer experiences. However, despite the clear benefits of software, traditional development methods can be time-consuming, costly, and often require a level of technical expertise that many businesses do not possess. This is where low-code and no-code platforms come into play, offering a new way for organizations to build applications quickly and efficiently without the need for extensive programming knowledge.

The need for low-code and no-code platforms arises from several key factors. First, businesses today operate in a highly dynamic environment where speed is critical. Markets move quickly, and companies must be able to adapt to changes in consumer behavior, technological advancements, and competitive pressures. In the past, developing software solutions to address these challenges required significant time and resources. Traditional development methods often involved lengthy planning, coding, and testing cycles that could take months or even years to complete. By the time a product or application was ready for deployment, it may have already been outdated or no longer aligned with the current needs of the business.

Low-code and no-code platforms are designed to address this issue by significantly reducing the time it takes to develop applications. These platforms provide visual, drag-and-drop interfaces that allow users to quickly assemble applications without writing extensive lines of code. By leveraging pre-built templates, components, and workflows, users can create applications that meet their needs with minimal effort. This speed of development is particularly important in today's fast-paced business world, where organizations cannot afford to wait for months to release new products or services.

Another critical factor driving the adoption of low-code and no-code platforms is the shortage of skilled developers. The demand for software development talent has been growing steadily for years, but the supply of qualified professionals has not kept pace. This skills gap has made it increasingly difficult for businesses to hire the developers they need to build and maintain custom applications. As a result, many organizations have found themselves facing long delays in their software development projects or forced to invest significant resources into training new developers.

Low-code and no-code platforms help mitigate this problem by enabling individuals with little or no technical experience to build applications. These platforms provide an intuitive user interface that guides users through the development process, making it accessible to people who may not have formal training in coding. This allows organizations to tap into a broader pool of talent, including business analysts, marketers, and operations professionals, who can now play an active role in the application development process. By empowering non-technical employees to create their own solutions, businesses can reduce their reliance on specialized developers and streamline the development process.

The democratization of application development through low-code and no-code platforms also promotes innovation. In traditional development models, the creation of new software ideas often depended on the expertise and resources of a small group of developers. As a result, many business units within organizations may have felt disconnected from the development process, leading to delays in addressing their specific needs. Low-code and no-code platforms change this dynamic by allowing business users to create applications that directly address their challenges. By giving employees the tools to build their own solutions, organizations encourage experimentation and foster a culture of innovation.

Additionally, low-code and no-code platforms can help businesses reduce costs. Traditional software development projects can be expensive, especially when factoring in the need for specialized developers, project managers, and IT infrastructure. Low-code and no-code platforms lower these costs by eliminating the need for extensive coding expertise and reducing the time required for development. This allows businesses to allocate their resources more efficiently and invest in other areas of growth. For small and medium-sized enterprises (SMEs), in particular, low-code and no-code platforms provide an affordable way to develop custom applications that might otherwise be out of reach due to financial constraints.

Beyond cost and speed, low-code and no-code platforms also address the challenge of integrating disparate systems. Many organizations rely on a variety of software tools and platforms to manage their operations, and these systems often do not communicate well with each other. Integrating these systems can be complex, expensive, and time-consuming, requiring specialized technical expertise. Low-code and no-code platforms make it easier to integrate data from various sources and create seamless workflows between applications. By providing built-in connectors and pre-configured integration options, these platforms allow users to build solutions that connect different systems without the need for custom coding.

The scalability and flexibility of low-code and no-code platforms also make them an attractive option for businesses looking to adapt to changing market conditions. As businesses grow and their needs evolve, they often require more sophisticated software solutions that can handle increased workloads or new functionality. While traditional development methods may require a complete overhaul of an existing system to accommodate these changes, low-code and no-code platforms allow for quicker updates and modifications. Users can easily tweak existing applications, add new features, or scale them up to handle larger volumes of data and users. This adaptability is particularly important in industries like healthcare, finance, and retail, where businesses must be able to respond quickly to changes in regulations, consumer preferences, and market trends.

Despite the many benefits, it is important to recognize that low-code and no-code platforms are not a one-size-fits-all solution. While they can handle many types of applications, there are still cases where custom-coded solutions are necessary. Complex applications that require highly specialized functionality, integrations, or performance optimizations may still need to be developed using traditional programming techniques. However, for many organizations, low-code and no-code platforms offer a practical and efficient way to address a wide range of business needs, from simple process automation to customer-facing applications.

The growing demand for digital transformation and the need for businesses to innovate quickly have made low-code and no-code platforms an essential tool in today's technology landscape. These platforms empower businesses to develop applications faster, with fewer resources, and by leveraging the skills of non-technical users. They also help to bridge the gap between IT and business departments, promoting collaboration and enabling organizations to respond more effectively to the demands of the modern market. As these platforms continue to evolve, they will likely become an even more integral part of the software development ecosystem, helping businesses stay competitive in an increasingly digital world.

The Evolution of Application Development

The field of application development has undergone a profound transformation over the past few decades. What once required complex, specialized skills and lengthy development cycles has become more accessible to a broader range of people. This evolution has been driven by technological advancements, changing business needs, and a growing demand for faster, more efficient software solutions. From the early days of manual coding to the modern era of low-code and no-code platforms, application development has evolved into a much more flexible and dynamic process, enabling organizations to adapt to changing market conditions and meet the growing demands of their users.

In the early days of application development, software was created by a small group of highly skilled developers using low-level programming languages. These languages, such as assembly and machine code, required developers to have a deep understanding of computer hardware and software architecture. Building applications was a labor-intensive process that involved writing every line of code from scratch. The development cycle was long, and the resulting software was often limited in functionality and prone to errors. Debugging and testing could take weeks or even months, and even small changes to the application required significant effort.

As technology progressed, high-level programming languages like C, Java, and Python emerged, making it easier for developers to create more sophisticated applications. These languages provided abstractions that allowed developers to focus on solving problems rather than worrying about the intricacies of computer hardware. However, even with these advancements, application development still required specialized knowledge and a significant amount of time and effort. The development process was often siloed, with different teams working on different parts of the application, which could lead to inefficiencies and delays.

With the rise of the internet and the advent of web-based applications in the late 1990s and early 2000s, the landscape of application development began to shift again. Web development technologies like HTML, CSS, and JavaScript opened up new possibilities for creating dynamic, interactive applications that could run in a web browser. This change not only expanded the types of applications that could be developed but also introduced the concept of cross-platform development, allowing applications to run on various devices and operating systems without the need for separate versions of the software.

The rise of web development also led to the emergence of frameworks and libraries designed to streamline the development process. Tools like Angular, React, and Django provided developers with pre-built components and templates that they could use to accelerate the development of web applications. While these frameworks still required a deep understanding of coding, they significantly reduced the time and effort needed to build complex applications. This shift allowed developers to focus more on the unique features and functionality of their applications rather than reinventing the wheel every time they started a new project.

As businesses increasingly relied on technology to drive their operations, the demand for custom applications grew. However, hiring skilled developers became more challenging, as the supply of qualified developers could not keep up with the demand. This shortage of technical talent led to a shift in the way organizations approached application development. Instead of relying solely on specialized developers, businesses began to explore ways to empower non-technical employees to contribute to the development process. This need for faster development and more accessible tools gave rise to the concept of low-code and no-code platforms.

Low-code and no-code platforms represent a significant departure from traditional development methods. These platforms allow users to create applications without writing extensive lines of code. Low-code platforms provide a visual interface with drag-and-drop components that enable users to design and build applications by configuring pre-built templates and workflows. No-code platforms take this concept even further by eliminating the need for any coding at all. These platforms offer fully visual tools that allow users to create applications through simple point-and-click interactions. The goal of these platforms is to democratize the development process, making it accessible to business users, analysts, and other non-technical individuals who may not have any experience with programming.

The rise of low-code and no-code platforms has transformed the way businesses approach application development. These platforms allow organizations to rapidly create applications that meet their specific needs, without having to rely on external developers or long development cycles. This accelerated development process has become increasingly important as businesses strive to keep up with the fast-paced demands of the market. With low-code and no-code platforms, organizations can quickly build prototypes, test new ideas, and launch applications that solve business problems in real-time. These platforms have become an essential tool for businesses seeking to stay competitive and agile in a rapidly changing landscape.

One of the driving forces behind the adoption of low-code and no-code platforms is the growing need for digital transformation. As organizations digitize their processes and move to the cloud, the demand for custom software solutions has skyrocketed. However, the traditional approach to development, which involves hiring specialized developers and managing complex projects, is no longer sustainable. Low-code and no-code platforms offer a more efficient way to meet the growing demand for custom applications while reducing costs and speeding up time to market. By enabling non-technical employees to participate in the development process, these platforms help organizations bridge the skills gap and create solutions that directly address their business needs.

The evolution of application development is also closely tied to the increasing reliance on cloud computing. Cloud-based platforms have made it easier for businesses to deploy and scale applications without the need for on-premises infrastructure. Cloud services provide the necessary resources to run applications at scale, allowing businesses to focus on building and optimizing their software rather than worrying about hardware and infrastructure. This shift to the cloud has made it possible for low-code and no-code platforms to thrive, as they rely on the scalability and flexibility of cloud infrastructure to deliver powerful, user-friendly applications.

As technology continues to evolve, the future of application development will likely be shaped by advancements in artificial intelligence (AI), machine learning (ML), and automation. These technologies have the potential to further simplify the development process by providing intelligent tools that can automatically generate code, suggest optimizations, and even detect and fix errors. The integration of AI and ML into low-code and no-code platforms could lead to even more sophisticated applications being built with minimal effort. These platforms will continue to evolve, providing businesses with even more powerful tools to create applications that meet their unique needs.

In the coming years, we are likely to see even more innovations in the field of application development. The boundaries between traditional development and low-code/no-code development will continue to blur as these platforms become more capable and integrated with other technologies. The future of application development will be defined by the increasing collaboration between developers and non-developers, with both groups working together to create solutions that drive business success. The evolution of application development is a testament to the power of innovation and the growing role of technology in shaping the future of business.

The Business Value of Low-Code/No-Code Solutions

In today's fast-paced business environment, organizations are increasingly seeking ways to streamline their operations and improve efficiency while keeping costs under control. Low-code and no-code solutions have emerged as powerful tools that provide substantial business value across various industries. These platforms enable businesses to rapidly develop and deploy applications without the need for extensive programming knowledge, empowering a broader range of employees to contribute to the development process. By removing technical barriers and reducing the time and resources required to create software, low-code and no-code solutions offer significant advantages that can enhance productivity, innovation, and agility in business operations.

One of the primary business benefits of low-code and no-code solutions is the speed at which applications can be developed. Traditional application development can be a lengthy process, often taking months or even years to design, build, test, and deploy. With the use of low-code and no-code platforms, development time is drastically reduced, allowing businesses to quickly launch new products, services, or features. This rapid development cycle is essential in a competitive market where time-to-market can be a critical factor in gaining a competitive advantage. Organizations can respond more quickly to changing customer needs, market demands, and emerging trends by accelerating the development process.

In addition to faster development, low-code and no-code platforms also provide significant cost savings. Traditional development projects typically require a team of skilled developers, project managers, and other technical resources, which can be costly for businesses, especially small and medium-sized enterprises (SMEs). By enabling non-technical employees, such as business analysts or operations managers, to build applications, these platforms reduce the need for highly specialized development resources. This not only cuts down on labor costs but also eliminates the need for extensive training or hiring of additional IT staff. As a result, businesses can allocate their resources more efficiently, focusing their budgets on other areas of growth and innovation.

Low-code and no-code platforms also allow organizations to bridge the skills gap that many businesses face. The demand for skilled developers has consistently outpaced the supply of qualified professionals, leaving many businesses struggling to find the talent they need to build and maintain custom applications. These platforms provide an opportunity for organizations to empower employees who may not have formal coding experience to participate in the development process. By democratizing application development, low-code and no-code platforms allow businesses to tap into a broader pool of talent and encourage greater collaboration between business and IT teams. This shift not only helps to address the talent shortage but also fosters a more collaborative and agile working environment.

The agility provided by low-code and no-code solutions is another valuable aspect for businesses. In today's ever-changing business landscape, organizations need to be able to adapt quickly to new opportunities, challenges, or regulatory changes. Low-code and no-code platforms make it easier for businesses to create custom solutions that address specific problems, without the long wait times associated with traditional development methods. If a business unit requires a new tool or application to streamline operations or meet customer demands, they can often build it themselves using these platforms, without waiting for IT to allocate resources. This ability to rapidly create and deploy applications empowers businesses to be more responsive and adaptive in a dynamic market.

Furthermore, the scalability and flexibility of low-code and no-code platforms make them a valuable asset for businesses of all sizes. As companies grow and their needs evolve, they often require more complex applications or additional features. Low-code and no-code platforms are designed to be highly flexible, allowing users to easily modify and scale applications as required. This scalability ensures that businesses can continue to use the same platform as their operations expand, avoiding the need for expensive and time-consuming redevelopment projects. Additionally, these platforms allow organizations to integrate new features, third-party services, or systems without significant additional development effort, making them a versatile tool for a variety of use cases.

The ability to automate processes is another key value proposition of low-code and no-code platforms. Many businesses rely on manual processes or outdated software systems that can lead to inefficiencies, errors, and delays. Low-code and no-code platforms enable organizations to automate workflows, integrate disparate systems, and streamline day-to-day operations. By automating repetitive tasks, businesses can reduce the risk of human error, improve consistency, and free up employees to focus on higher-value activities. Workflow automation is especially important in areas such as customer service, inventory management, and human resources, where efficiency gains can have a significant impact on the bottom line.

In addition to improving operational efficiency, low-code and no-code platforms also foster innovation within organizations. Traditionally, the development of new software solutions was confined to a small group of developers who had the skills and resources to build custom applications. Low-code and no-code platforms allow business users to create their own solutions, encouraging experimentation and creative problem-solving. This democratization of development helps organizations to uncover new ideas and processes that might not have been considered otherwise. Employees who are closest to the day-to-day operations are often in the best position to identify inefficiencies or opportunities for improvement, and low-code and no-code platforms give them the tools to act on those insights quickly.

The use of low-code and no-code solutions can also improve the customer experience. Many businesses today are focused on enhancing their customer-facing applications, whether it's through more intuitive user interfaces, personalized services, or faster response times. Low-code and no-code platforms allow organizations to quickly build and iterate on customer-facing applications, ensuring that they meet customer expectations in real-time. The ability to rapidly launch updates, add new features, or address issues ensures that businesses can provide a seamless, high-quality experience for their users.

Security and compliance are also important considerations for businesses, especially in industries such as healthcare, finance, and government. Low-code and no-code platforms are increasingly offering robust security features to protect sensitive data and ensure compliance with regulations. These platforms provide businesses with built-in security tools such as encryption, user authentication, and role-based access control, which help to mitigate security risks. By leveraging these features, businesses can ensure that their applications meet industry standards and protect customer and organizational data.

As organizations continue to adopt low-code and no-code platforms, they will be better positioned to stay competitive in an increasingly digital world. These solutions provide businesses with the agility, cost savings, and innovation needed to thrive in a fast-paced market. By empowering non-technical users to participate in the development process, businesses can unlock new opportunities and deliver better, more tailored solutions to their customers. The value of low-code and no-code solutions extends far beyond simple application development, as these platforms contribute to overall business growth, transformation, and success.

Core Concepts of Low-Code/No-Code Platforms

Low-code and no-code platforms have revolutionized the way software applications are developed. By offering intuitive, visual development tools, these platforms empower users with little to no technical expertise to create, modify, and deploy applications quickly and efficiently. The core concepts behind low-code and no-code platforms are centered around simplifying the development process, enabling faster delivery of business solutions, and promoting innovation across a wide range of industries. To understand the value of these platforms, it is essential to explore their fundamental concepts, which include visual development, drag-and-drop functionality, reusable components, integrations, and automation.

At the heart of low-code and no-code platforms is the idea of visual development. Traditional software development typically involves writing lines of code to create functionality. In contrast, low-code and no-code platforms rely heavily on graphical user interfaces (GUIs) that enable users to design applications visually. These platforms provide a drag-and-drop interface that allows users to place components like buttons, text fields, and other UI elements onto a canvas, positioning them in a way that reflects the desired structure of the application. Instead of focusing on syntax and coding logic, users can concentrate on the application's flow and user experience. This visual approach reduces the complexity of development, allowing business users, who may not have a background in coding, to create functional applications without needing to write a single line of code.

Drag-and-drop functionality is one of the defining features of low-code and no-code platforms. This functionality simplifies the process of assembling applications by allowing users to simply drag components from a palette and drop them into the application's design. These components can include everything from UI elements like buttons and text boxes to more complex components such as workflows, database connections, and integration modules. The simplicity of drag-and-drop interaction makes it accessible to individuals with minimal technical skills. The process is intuitive, reducing the learning curve and enabling users to create applications quickly and efficiently. As a result, organizations can expedite their application development cycles, delivering solutions to market faster than ever before.

Another key concept in low-code and no-code platforms is the use of reusable components. These components are pre-built blocks of code or functionality that can be used across different applications. Reusable components can range from simple UI elements like form fields to more complex features such as data validation, payment gateways, or even entire business workflows. The ability to reuse components helps standardize development across an organization and ensures consistency across applications. It also speeds up the development process, as users do not have to reinvent the wheel every time they build an application. By leveraging a library of pre-built components, developers and business users alike can save time and effort, allowing them to focus on customizing the application to meet their specific needs.

Integrations are another critical concept in low-code and no-code platforms. In today's business environment, most organizations rely on a variety of software tools and systems to manage their operations. Whether it's customer relationship management (CRM) software, enterprise resource planning (ERP) systems, or marketing platforms, these tools need to communicate with one another to ensure data flows seamlessly across the organization. Low-code and no-code platforms make it easier to integrate these systems through pre-built connectors or integration modules. These connectors allow users to link their applications to external data sources, APIs, or third-party services without the need for custom coding. By simplifying the integration process, these platforms enable organizations to create applications that work in harmony with their existing technology ecosystem, reducing the complexity of managing multiple systems.

Automation is another fundamental concept within low-code and no-code platforms. Many business processes involve repetitive tasks that can be time-consuming and prone to human error. Low-code and no-code platforms provide users with the tools to automate these tasks, creating workflows that can handle everything from data entry to complex decision-making processes. For example, a user can create an automated workflow that sends an email notification when a certain condition is met, or one that automatically updates a database when new information is entered. Automation can significantly improve operational efficiency by eliminating manual steps, reducing errors, and ensuring that tasks are completed in a timely and consistent manner. This capability is particularly useful in industries where efficiency is critical, such as finance, healthcare, and retail.

One of the most compelling aspects of low-code and no-code platforms is their ability to enable collaboration between business users and IT departments. In traditional development environments, there is often a divide between business users, who have intimate knowledge of the company's needs, and IT professionals, who possess the technical skills to build software solutions. Low-code and no-code platforms bridge this gap by allowing business users to participate directly in the development process. With these platforms, business users can build or modify applications to meet their specific needs without relying on developers. IT departments still play an important role in overseeing the development process, ensuring that security, scalability, and compliance requirements are met, but the involvement of business users fosters greater alignment between the business's goals and the solutions being developed.

The concept of governance is also essential in low-code and no-code platforms. While these platforms enable rapid application development, it is crucial to ensure that the applications being built are secure, reliable, and aligned with organizational standards. Low-code and no-code platforms often include governance tools that allow organizations to monitor and control the development process. These tools help ensure that applications adhere to best practices, comply with regulatory requirements, and follow the organization's security policies. Governance features may include role-based access controls, audit trails, and version control, all of which provide transparency and accountability in the development process. By incorporating governance into the platform, organizations can maintain oversight while still enabling a more agile approach to application development.

Low-code and no-code platforms are also designed to be scalable. While they are ideal for building simple applications, these platforms can also support more complex use cases as organizations grow. The scalability of these platforms ensures that applications can handle increased user traffic, larger data sets, and more complex workflows as the organization's needs evolve. Additionally, these platforms allow for seamless upgrades and expansions, enabling businesses to continuously improve their applications without the need for complete redevelopment. The ability to scale applications without compromising performance or reliability is critical for businesses that need to keep pace with growth and innovation.

The core concepts of low-code and no-code platforms—visual development, drag-and-drop functionality, reusable components, integrations, automation, collaboration, governance, and scalability—combine to offer a compelling solution for modern application development. By empowering business users, accelerating development cycles, and providing flexibility and scalability, these platforms are transforming the way organizations create and deploy software. As businesses continue to embrace digital transformation, low-code and no-code platforms are likely to play an increasingly important role in shaping the future of application development.

How Low-Code/No-Code Development Works

Low-code and no-code development represent a transformative approach to creating software applications, focusing on reducing the complexity of traditional development processes and making application building accessible to a broader range of users. These platforms provide a visual environment in which users can design and implement applications with minimal or no coding at all, relying instead on intuitive tools and pre-built components. The core of low-code and no-code platforms is the ability to abstract much of the technical complexity involved in application development, allowing individuals with little to no programming knowledge to participate in creating functional, scalable applications. Understanding how these platforms work requires an exploration of the various components and workflows that define their operation.

At the heart of low-code and no-code platforms is the visual development environment. Unlike traditional development environments, where developers write lines of code in programming languages like Java or Python, low-code and no-code platforms provide a graphical interface where users can drag and drop components to design their applications. These components are pre-built elements, such as buttons, text fields, dropdown menus, and other user interface elements, that can be easily positioned and customized within the visual design interface. This approach allows users to focus on the application's functionality and user experience, without needing to worry about the underlying code. By providing a more accessible interface, these platforms enable non-technical users, such as business analysts or operations managers, to build applications that solve real-world problems.

In addition to visual design, low-code and no-code platforms offer a wide range of pre-built templates and components that users can integrate into their applications. These templates can be used as starting points for building applications, saving users significant time and effort. For example, there might be a pre-built template for a customer relationship management (CRM) system, an inventory management application, or a simple e-commerce site. These templates often come with default workflows and logic already built-in, allowing users to customize them further to meet specific business requirements. This approach significantly accelerates the development process, as users do not need to build everything from scratch. They can modify and adjust the templates to suit their needs, all within the platform's visual interface.

The underlying logic of low-code and no-code applications is built using visual workflows rather than traditional programming. In a typical low-code environment, users can define business logic and workflows by configuring rules or creating decision trees within the platform. This process involves specifying how data should flow between different components or systems and establishing the conditions under which specific actions should occur. For example, a user might set up a workflow that automatically sends an email notification when a particular condition is met or one that updates a database when a form is submitted. These workflows are usually defined using a simple, intuitive interface where users can select from a range of pre-defined actions and connect them in a sequence. This abstraction allows non-developers to create sophisticated business logic without needing to write any code.

No-code platforms take this approach even further by eliminating the need for any coding altogether. In no-code environments, users can configure complex workflows, integrations, and logic entirely through visual tools. Everything from database connections to third-party service integrations can be handled using point-and-click interactions. No-code platforms often include pre-configured connectors that allow users to integrate their applications with external systems, such as CRM software, payment gateways, or cloud storage solutions, all without writing any code. This makes it easier for organizations to create custom solutions that integrate seamlessly with their existing technology stack.

Another essential aspect of low-code and no-code development is the ability to create and manage databases without the need for complex database management skills. In traditional development, managing databases often involves writing SQL queries, defining table structures, and ensuring data integrity. In low-code and no-code platforms, users can create and manage databases through simple forms and interfaces. These platforms usually provide a built-in database where users can define tables, fields, and relationships between different data entities, all within the platform's graphical interface. This simplifies the process of building data-driven applications and enables users to focus on the functionality of the application itself rather than the intricacies of database management.

Integration with external systems is another area where low-code and no-code platforms excel. Many business applications rely on data from multiple sources, such as customer data from CRM systems, financial data from accounting software, or inventory data from supply chain management systems. Low-code and no-code platforms often come with pre-built connectors that allow users to integrate their applications with popular third-party services and APIs. This eliminates the need for developers to write complex integration code and allows businesses to create custom solutions that pull data from multiple sources. For instance, a no-code platform might allow a user to integrate their inventory management system with a supplier's API to automatically reorder products when stock levels are low, all through simple configuration settings.

Security and governance are also critical components in how low-code and no-code platforms operate. While these platforms make it easier for non-technical users to create applications, they still incorporate features to ensure that applications are secure and compliant with industry regulations. Many low-code and no-code platforms come with built-in authentication and authorization features, such as role-based access controls, ensuring that only authorized users can access certain parts of the application. Additionally, platforms often include audit trails, version control, and other governance tools that enable organizations to track changes to applications and ensure that they meet security and compliance standards. These features help mitigate the risks associated with empowering business users to create applications, ensuring that they do not compromise the integrity of the organization's data or systems.

Scalability is another consideration for low-code and no-code development platforms. While these platforms are designed to handle a wide range of applications, from simple internal tools to more complex enterprise solutions, scalability is a key factor in their functionality. Many low-code and no-code platforms are built on cloud infrastructure, which means they can scale dynamically as the demands on the application increase. Users can add additional features, increase data storage, or handle higher volumes of traffic without worrying about managing servers or infrastructure. This makes low-code and no-code platforms suitable for organizations of all sizes, from small startups to large enterprises.

Despite their accessibility and ease of use, low-code and no-code platforms do have limitations. While these platforms enable the rapid development of many types of applications, they may not be suitable for highly complex or highly specialized projects that require custom code. In these cases, developers may still need to write traditional code to implement specific features or performance optimizations. However, for the majority of use cases, low-code and no-code platforms offer a compelling alternative to traditional development, providing a faster, more efficient way to build applications that meet business needs.

Low-code and no-code development works by simplifying the process of creating software applications, making it accessible to non-technical users while still offering the flexibility and power required for more complex solutions. Through visual interfaces, pre-built components, automated workflows, and seamless integrations, these platforms enable users to design, build, and deploy applications with minimal coding effort. Whether for simple internal tools or more sophisticated business applications, low-code and no-code platforms provide a user-friendly environment that reduces the barriers to entry for application development and accelerates the creation of software solutions.

The Key Components of Low-Code/No-Code Platforms

Low-code and no-code platforms have transformed the landscape of software development by simplifying the process of creating applications. These platforms enable users, regardless of their technical background, to design, build, and deploy software applications with little to no coding involved. At the core of these platforms are several key components that work together to facilitate the rapid development and deployment of functional, scalable applications. Understanding these components helps clarify how low-code and no-code platforms operate and why they have become so popular in the business world.

One of the fundamental components of low-code and no-code platforms is the visual development environment. Unlike traditional coding, which requires developers to write detailed lines of code, the visual development environment provides a graphical interface that allows users to design applications by dragging and dropping pre-built components onto a canvas. This visual approach simplifies the application-building process, allowing users to focus on the overall design and functionality of their application without getting bogged down in the complexities of programming syntax. Through this interface, users can configure the structure, layout, and flow of their application, all within a single cohesive environment. By providing a more intuitive way to design applications, the visual environment makes application development accessible to business users, entrepreneurs, and others who may not have formal coding expertise.

Another key component is the library of pre-built components and templates that low-code and no-code platforms offer. These platforms come with a range of reusable components, such as buttons, input fields, navigation menus, and other user interface (UI) elements, that can be quickly integrated into the application. In addition to UI components, platforms often include more complex elements like data models, workflows, integrations, and logic functions. These components are pre-designed and optimized to work seamlessly within the platform, allowing users to assemble applications quickly without needing to build each element from scratch. For example, a user could choose a template for a customer relationship management (CRM) application and then customize it to fit their specific business needs. By providing a library of reusable components, low-code and no-code platforms save users significant time and effort, making the application development process much more efficient.

Workflows and automation are also essential components of these platforms. Workflows define the sequence of actions or steps that an application will perform in response to user input or external events. In traditional development, creating workflows often involves writing complex code to define how data should be processed, validated, and transferred. In low-code and no-code platforms, users can create workflows by visually connecting different actions or steps. For example, a user could create a workflow that triggers an email notification when a form is submitted or updates a database when new data is entered. These workflows can be highly customizable, allowing users to create complex business logic without the need for programming knowledge. Automation capabilities further enhance this by enabling repetitive tasks to be completed without manual intervention. Through automation, businesses can streamline their processes, reduce errors, and ensure that tasks are completed in a timely manner.

Data management is another critical component of low-code and no-code platforms. Many applications require robust data storage and management capabilities to handle the information users input or interact with. These platforms provide built-in tools for managing data, such as databases or data tables, which users can configure and manipulate through simple interfaces. Users can create data models, define relationships between different data entities, and set up processes for retrieving, updating, and deleting records. In addition, many low-code and no-code platforms offer built-in integrations with external databases or data sources, allowing users to connect their applications to cloud services, CRM systems, or other enterprise software tools. This integration simplifies the process of managing and accessing data, enabling users to build data-driven applications without needing to have expertise in database management or SQL.

Integrations with third-party services are also a core component of low-code and no-code platforms. In today's interconnected world, businesses often rely on a variety of external services and software tools to manage their operations. Whether it's a payment gateway, a marketing platform, or a customer service tool, integrating these services with internal applications is crucial for ensuring smooth operations. Low-code and no-code platforms come equipped with pre-built connectors and APIs that allow users to easily integrate their applications with third-party services. This eliminates the need for writing custom code to handle integrations and allows users to quickly connect their applications to popular services like Salesforce, Google Analytics, or Stripe. These connectors provide a seamless way to exchange data between systems, enabling businesses to automate workflows, improve efficiency, and reduce the risk of errors.

User authentication and security are also important components of low-code and no-code platforms. As with any software application, it is essential to ensure that only authorized users can access sensitive data or perform specific actions within the application. Low-code and no-code platforms include security features that help safeguard applications from unauthorized access. These features often include user authentication mechanisms, such as single sign-on (SSO), multi-factor authentication (MFA), and role-based access controls (RBAC), which allow administrators to control who can access different parts of the application. By providing these built-in security features, platforms make it easier for businesses to create secure applications that comply with industry standards and regulations without requiring deep technical knowledge of security protocols.

Deployment and scalability are also key components of low-code and no-code platforms. Once an application is developed, it must be deployed to a server or cloud infrastructure so that it can be accessed by users. Low-code and no-code platforms typically include simple deployment tools that allow users to publish their applications with just a few clicks. These tools often include built-in hosting or integration with cloud services like AWS or Azure, making it easy to deploy applications without needing to manage servers or infrastructure. Additionally, scalability is an important consideration as businesses grow. Low-code and no-code platforms are often built on cloud infrastructure, which allows applications to scale easily by adding more resources as demand increases. This cloud-based architecture ensures that applications remain responsive and reliable, even as the number of users or the amount of data grows.

Finally, analytics and reporting are crucial components of low-code and no-code platforms. As businesses use their applications, it's essential to track performance, monitor usage, and analyze data to make informed decisions. Many platforms include built-in analytics tools that provide insights into how the application is being used and how it is performing. These tools can generate reports on metrics such as user engagement, conversion rates, and process efficiency. By having access to real-time analytics, businesses can quickly identify areas for improvement and make adjustments to optimize their applications for better performance and user experience.

The key components of low-code and no-code platforms work together to provide an environment where users can quickly and efficiently create, deploy, and manage applications. From visual development environments and pre-built components to automation, data management, and third-party integrations, these platforms simplify the development process and empower a broader range of users to contribute to software creation. By providing tools for security, deployment, and scalability, low-code and no-code platforms ensure that applications are secure, reliable, and capable of meeting the needs of growing businesses. The combination of these components makes low-code and no-code platforms a powerful and versatile solution for organizations seeking to build custom applications without relying on traditional development methods.

Building Applications Without Code: The Basics

Building applications without writing a single line of code is one of the most revolutionary aspects of modern software development. The introduction of no-code platforms has transformed the way businesses and individuals approach application creation, making it possible for those without technical backgrounds to design, develop, and deploy powerful applications. These platforms provide a simplified development environment, where users can rely on visual interfaces and drag-and-drop features to create functional applications, all without the need for programming knowledge. Understanding the basics of building applications without code involves exploring how these platforms work and the fundamental tools they offer to make application development accessible to everyone.

At its core, no-code development is about eliminating the need for traditional coding. Instead of writing custom scripts and defining the logic of an application through code, users interact with a graphical user interface (GUI) that allows them to design and configure their application. This GUI often includes drag-and-drop elements like buttons, text fields, and menus, as well as more complex components such as workflows, data models, and integrations with third-party services. The visual approach to building applications means that users can focus on what they want their application to do and how they want it to look, without worrying about the syntax or structure of the underlying code.

One of the most important aspects of building applications without code is the use of templates. No-code platforms typically offer a library of pre-built templates that users can select and customize to meet their needs. These templates can range from simple forms and to-do lists to more complex business solutions like customer relationship management (CRM) systems, inventory management tools, or e-commerce websites. The templates provide a solid foundation for users to start their application development, and they can be tailored through the no-code platform's intuitive interface. By leveraging these templates, users can avoid the process of building an application from scratch, saving considerable time and effort. These templates also often come with pre-configured business logic and workflows that automate common tasks, allowing users to focus on customizing the application rather than building out basic functionality.

Once a template is chosen, the next step in building an application without code is customizing the user interface (UI). The UI is the part of the application that users interact with directly, and it plays a crucial role in the overall user experience. In a no-code platform, the user interface is created visually, with components being dragged and dropped into place on a canvas. Users can adjust the layout, change colors, resize elements, and add interactivity without needing to write any HTML, CSS, or JavaScript. The no-code platform handles the technical aspects of ensuring that the UI components function as intended, such as making sure buttons trigger the correct actions or that forms send data to the right place. This level of customization allows users to create a tailored application that suits their business needs, while also maintaining an intuitive, user-friendly design.

Alongside the visual design, workflows are another key component of building applications without code. Workflows define the sequence of actions or tasks that an application will perform based on user inputs or other events. In traditional application development, these workflows would be defined by writing custom logic in code, which requires a deep understanding of programming. However, no-code platforms allow users to create workflows through simple visual interfaces. By dragging and connecting different actions, users can define how their application responds to specific inputs. For example, if a user fills out a form, the workflow might dictate that the application sends an email confirmation, saves the data to a database, and updates a dashboard. These workflows can also include conditions, such as only triggering an action if certain criteria are met, enabling users to build more complex business logic without writing a single line of code.

Data management is another essential component in building applications without code. Many applications, especially business solutions, require a backend database to store and retrieve information. No-code platforms provide users with tools to create and manage databases visually. Users can define tables, fields, and relationships between different types of data without needing to write SQL queries or configure database servers. For instance, if a user is building a CRM application, they might create a table to store customer information, including fields for the customer's name, contact details, and purchase history. No-code platforms also allow users to create forms for inputting data into these tables and establish rules for how data is validated, ensuring that users input accurate and consistent information. The no-code platform handles the complexity of database management in the background, enabling users to focus on the application's functionality rather than its technical infrastructure.

Integration with external services is another powerful feature of no-code platforms. In many cases, an application needs to interact with other systems, such as payment processors, email services, or cloud storage providers. Writing custom code to integrate these services can be complex and time-consuming, but no-code platforms simplify the process by providing pre-built connectors to popular third-party services. For example, a user building an e-commerce application might need to integrate a payment gateway like Stripe or PayPal. In a no-code environment, they can do this by simply selecting the relevant integration from a list and entering the necessary credentials. These integrations allow the application to communicate with external systems without requiring the user to write any API calls or handle the underlying technical details. The platform takes care of managing the integration, ensuring that the application works seamlessly with other tools.

Security is always a concern when building applications, and no-code platforms are no exception. While these platforms simplify the development process, they also include built-in security features to ensure that the applications created are secure and compliant with industry standards. Many no-code platforms offer features like user authentication, role-based access control, and data encryption to protect sensitive information. Users can set up these security features through the platform's interface, without needing to worry about the technical aspects of implementing secure login systems or encrypting data at rest. These security features make no-code platforms a viable option for creating applications that handle sensitive information, such as customer data or financial records, while still ensuring that the application is protected from unauthorized access.

Once an application is built, no-code platforms also provide tools for deploying and maintaining the application. Deploying an application typically involves setting up servers, configuring hosting environments, and ensuring that the application is accessible to users. No-code platforms take care of much of this for users, allowing them to deploy their application with just a few clicks. Many platforms also offer cloud hosting services, meaning users do not need to worry about managing infrastructure. The no-code platform ensures that the application is hosted securely and is available to users on demand.

Building applications without code offers a new way for individuals and businesses to create custom solutions without relying on developers or specialized technical knowledge. By providing intuitive, visual development tools, no-code platforms allow users to design user interfaces, automate workflows, manage data, integrate with third-party services, and deploy applications, all without writing a single line of code. The simplicity of these platforms opens up the world of software development to a much broader audience, empowering people to create solutions that meet their specific needs quickly and efficiently. This shift in how applications are built is reshaping the way businesses approach software development, enabling faster innovation and a more democratized approach to technology.

Choosing the Right Low-Code/No-Code Platform

The rise of low-code and no-code platforms has opened up new possibilities for organizations to develop applications quickly and efficiently, often without relying on traditional software development expertise. With the growing number of these platforms available, businesses and individuals seeking to build custom applications face the challenge of selecting the right one to meet their needs. Choosing the right low-code or no-code platform involves considering several factors, including the platform's functionality, scalability, user-friendliness, integrations, and security features. By evaluating these factors, organizations can ensure that they choose a platform that aligns with their goals and delivers the most value.

One of the first things to consider when choosing a low-code or no-code platform is the type of application being built. Different platforms are designed to cater to different use cases, and understanding the requirements of the application will guide the selection process. For instance, some platforms specialize in building simple applications, such as forms or task management tools, while others are more suited for complex applications that involve workflows, integrations, and advanced data management. It is important to evaluate the platform's capabilities in relation to the scope of the application. A platform that excels in building mobile apps may not be the best choice for developing enterprise-level applications, and vice versa. Thus, businesses must ensure that the platform they choose offers the right set of features to handle their specific use case.

User-friendliness is another critical factor when selecting a low-code or no-code platform. These platforms are designed to make application development accessible to users without technical expertise, but not all platforms are created equal in terms of ease of use. Some platforms feature intuitive drag-and-drop interfaces, visual builders, and pre-built templates, which make the development process straightforward and fast. Others may require more configuration or have steeper learning curves, which could slow down the development process and hinder user adoption. It is important to evaluate how easy it is for users, especially those without coding experience, to navigate and use the platform. A user-friendly platform will ensure that business users can take full advantage of the tools available to them and will facilitate collaboration between IT teams and non-technical users.

Scalability is a crucial consideration, especially for businesses that plan to grow over time. As organizations expand, the applications they use often need to evolve to meet new demands, such as increased user traffic, more data, or additional features. The platform should be able to support these changes without requiring a complete overhaul of the application. Some low-code and no-code platforms offer the ability to scale applications seamlessly by leveraging cloud infrastructure, while others may have limitations that require additional development or customization to accommodate growth. It is essential to assess the scalability of the platform to ensure that it can handle increased workloads and adapt to future business needs. Additionally, organizations should consider how easy it is to upgrade or modify applications as they scale, as this can impact long-term maintenance and flexibility.

Another important aspect of choosing the right platform is the integration capabilities it offers. In most business environments, applications need to communicate with other software systems, such as customer relationship management (CRM) tools, enterprise resource planning (ERP) systems, or cloud storage services. A good low-code or no-code platform should provide built-in integrations with these popular third-party systems, allowing users to easily connect their applications to external data sources and services. Integration capabilities are particularly important for organizations that need to streamline their workflows, automate processes, or ensure that their applications work in tandem with other tools in their tech stack. Evaluating the range and ease of integrations offered by a platform is essential to ensure that it can meet the connectivity requirements of the organization.

Security is always a top priority when building applications, particularly when handling sensitive data such as customer information, financial records, or personal identifiers. When choosing a low-code or no-code platform, businesses must ensure that it provides robust security features to protect data and ensure compliance with industry regulations. Many platforms offer built-in security mechanisms, such as user authentication, encryption, and role-based access controls, which help safeguard applications from unauthorized access. It is important to assess how well the platform aligns with security best practices, including data protection laws such as the General Data Protection Regulation (GDPR) or Health Insurance Portability and Accountability Act (HIPAA). A secure platform will minimize the risk of data breaches and ensure that the applications built on it are compliant with the necessary legal and regulatory frameworks.

Cost is another key factor in the decision-making process. While low-code and no-code platforms generally offer cost savings compared to traditional development methods, the pricing models for these platforms can vary significantly. Some platforms charge based on the number of users, the features included, or the amount of data stored, while others may have subscription-based pricing or tiered packages.

It is important for organizations to consider their budget and how the pricing structure aligns with their expected usage and growth. A platform that offers a low initial cost may become more expensive as the application scales or as additional features are required. Therefore, businesses should carefully evaluate the long-term costs of the platform, including any potential hidden fees, to ensure that it fits within their financial plans.

Support and community are also vital considerations when choosing a platform. As with any software, users may encounter challenges or require assistance during the development process. A platform that provides excellent customer support, training resources, and a robust user community can significantly enhance the development experience. Many low-code and no-code platforms offer access to online tutorials, knowledge bases, and forums where users can seek help or share tips and best practices. Additionally, some platforms provide dedicated support teams to assist with technical issues or troubleshooting. Access to reliable support can ensure that users do not encounter roadblocks that could delay the development of their application.

Customization and flexibility are also worth considering. While no-code platforms are designed to minimize the need for custom code, some businesses may require more advanced features or customization that go beyond the pre-built components available. In such cases, it is essential to evaluate how much customization the platform allows. Some low-code platforms offer greater flexibility, enabling users to write custom code or integrate third-party modules to extend the functionality of their applications. This flexibility is crucial for businesses that need more tailored solutions or that plan to add advanced features in the future. It is important to find a balance between the platform's ease of use and the level of customization it allows, as this will determine whether it can accommodate both simple and complex requirements.

Finally, businesses should consider the reputation and longevity of the platform provider. As with any software, it is important to choose a platform from a provider with a strong track record and ongoing commitment to innovation and customer support. A platform from a reputable provider is more likely to receive regular updates, new features, and continued improvements, ensuring that it remains competitive and reliable over time. Researching user reviews, case studies, and success stories can provide valuable insights into the platform's performance and its ability to meet the needs of businesses similar to one's own.

Choosing the right low-code or no-code platform requires careful consideration of a variety of factors, from functionality and scalability to security and cost. By evaluating these key aspects, organizations can select a platform that aligns with their specific needs and ensures the successful development and deployment of applications. With the right platform, businesses can accelerate their digital transformation, improve operational efficiency, and empower their teams to create innovative solutions without relying on traditional software development methods.

User Interface Design in Low-Code/No-Code Development

User interface (UI) design plays a crucial role in the development of any application, as it directly influences the user experience. In low-code and no-code development environments, UI design becomes an essential aspect of building applications that are not only functional but also intuitive and visually appealing. These platforms offer a simplified approach to UI design, allowing individuals with little to no coding knowledge to create user-friendly applications. Despite the ease of use that these platforms offer, designing a compelling UI requires an understanding of basic design principles and how they can be effectively implemented within the limitations and possibilities of a no-code environment.

In a traditional development setting, creating a UI often requires a detailed understanding of front-end development technologies like HTML, CSS, and JavaScript. These languages allow developers to build the structure, layout, and interactive elements of an application's interface. However, low-code and no-code platforms abstract much of this complexity, providing users with visual design tools that allow them to create and customize their UI with little or no coding required. Through drag-and-drop components, templates, and pre-configured elements, users can design interfaces that meet the needs of their target audience without having to write any code.

One of the main advantages of using a low-code or no-code platform for UI design is the speed at which applications can be developed. Traditional UI design often involves a lengthy process of coding, testing, and debugging. With low-code/no-code platforms, this process is significantly shortened. Users can quickly assemble elements such as buttons, text fields, images, and forms into a cohesive layout, making it possible to develop functional prototypes and fully-fledged applications in a fraction of the time it would take using traditional coding methods. The availability of pre-built templates, along with ready-to-use components, further accelerates the design process. These templates are often designed to meet common user needs, such as building a login page, a registration form, or an e-commerce checkout interface, allowing users to build applications that are not only quick to develop but also built on proven design principles.

However, while these platforms offer a simplified approach to UI design, it is still essential to maintain a focus on usability and user-centered design. The primary goal of UI design is to create an experience that is intuitive, easy to navigate, and visually appealing. In low-code and no-code development, achieving this goal requires a thoughtful approach to the arrangement of elements on the page. For example, buttons should be placed in locations that are easy to reach and logically aligned with the flow of the application. Forms should be simple, with clear labels and instructions to guide users through the process. The layout of the page should be designed with the end-user in mind, ensuring that they can easily find the information or functionality they are seeking without unnecessary complexity.

An essential component of UI design in low-code and no-code platforms is customization. While these platforms provide a wide range of pre-built components and templates, it is essential for users to be able to adjust these elements to fit the unique needs of their application. Customizing the look and feel of the interface is crucial to ensuring that the application aligns with the branding and style guidelines of the organization or business it is being built for. Most low-code and no-code platforms offer design options for altering colors, fonts, sizes, and layouts. Users can customize the style of individual components or the entire page, allowing them to create a consistent and professional appearance. Additionally, these platforms often support the inclusion of images, logos, and other multimedia elements, further enhancing the visual appeal of the application.

Responsiveness is another important aspect of UI design that must be considered when developing applications in low-code and no-code platforms. In today's digital world, applications must function across a variety of devices and screen sizes, from desktop computers to smartphones and tablets. Many low-code and no-code platforms come with built-in responsive design features, ensuring that the layout of the application automatically adjusts to different screen sizes. This eliminates the need for users to manually code for responsiveness, as the platform handles much of the work behind the scenes. However, it is still essential for users to test their designs on various devices to ensure that the application provides a consistent experience for all users. By leveraging the responsive design features of these platforms, developers can ensure that their applications are accessible and functional on any device.

While UI design in low-code and no-code development offers significant advantages in terms of speed and accessibility, it also presents certain limitations. One of the challenges of working within these platforms is the lack of full control over every aspect of the design. In traditional development, developers can create custom UI elements and interactions from scratch, allowing them to fine-tune every aspect of the interface. In contrast, low-code and no-code platforms may offer a more limited set of components and features, which can restrict the level of customization that is possible. For example, some platforms may not allow users to create highly customized animations or complex interactive elements without resorting to custom code. While these limitations are generally manageable for most business applications, they can be a challenge for projects that require more advanced UI design.

Another challenge of UI design in low-code and no-code platforms is ensuring that the user interface remains accessible to all users, including those with disabilities. Accessibility is a critical aspect of design that ensures that applications are usable by people with varying abilities. Low-code and no-code platforms typically provide basic accessibility features, such as keyboard navigation and screen reader compatibility, but users still need to be mindful of accessibility best practices when designing their applications. This includes ensuring that text is legible, color contrast is sufficient, and that interactive elements are easy to interact with. By taking accessibility into account, users can create applications that are inclusive and usable by a broader audience.

User testing is a key part of UI design, regardless of whether an application is developed using traditional coding or low-code/no-code tools. Even though these platforms make it easier to build applications, it is essential to test the user interface to identify any potential usability issues or design flaws. Conducting usability testing allows developers to gather feedback from actual users and make adjustments to the UI based on their experiences. This iterative process is crucial for ensuring that the application is as user-friendly as possible and that it meets the needs of the target audience. Low-code and no-code platforms facilitate this testing by enabling quick updates and modifications to the design, which can be immediately tested and improved upon.

Designing a user interface in a low-code or no-code development environment requires an understanding of design principles, user needs, and the capabilities of the platform itself. While these platforms provide an accessible way to create applications without needing to write code, the design process still requires careful consideration of usability, customization, responsiveness, and accessibility. By using the tools and features provided by these platforms, developers and business users alike can create applications that are visually appealing, functional, and user-friendly, all while maintaining a fast and efficient development cycle.

Integrating Data Sources in Low-Code/No-Code Platforms

In the modern world of application development, the ability to integrate data from various sources is critical to creating functional, dynamic applications. In traditional development, data integration typically involves writing complex code to connect different systems, retrieve information, and present it in a meaningful way. However, low-code and no-code platforms have simplified this process, enabling users to connect to a variety of data sources without needing advanced programming skills. This has significantly accelerated the development process, allowing businesses to create data-driven applications quickly while also making it easier to integrate and manage the flow of data across various systems. Understanding how data integration works in these platforms and the components involved is essential for leveraging their full potential.

The heart of data integration in low-code and no-code platforms is the use of connectors. Connectors are pre-built modules that facilitate the connection between the platform and external data sources. These data sources can be anything from relational databases like MySQL and PostgreSQL to cloud services like Google Sheets, Salesforce, or even social media platforms like Facebook and Twitter. In traditional development, integrating with these sources would require writing custom API calls or complex queries. Low-code and no-code platforms eliminate this need by providing simple, user-friendly interfaces that allow users to link their applications to external data sources with just a few clicks. The connectors are designed to manage the complexities of authentication, data retrieval, and error handling behind the scenes, so the user can focus on how the data is used within the application.

One of the key advantages of using low-code and no-code platforms for data integration is the speed with which users can connect and use data from different sources. Traditionally, integrating data could take weeks or months, particularly if custom development was required. With low-code and no-code platforms, these integrations can often be completed in a matter of hours or days. This speed is crucial for businesses that need to quickly deploy solutions, respond to changing market conditions, or innovate in a fast-paced digital landscape. The ability to quickly integrate various data sources means that organizations can create applications that pull real-time data, synchronize information across systems, and automate processes in a fraction of the time it would take using traditional methods.

Beyond connecting to databases and cloud services, low-code and no-code platforms also allow users to integrate data through APIs. APIs, or application programming interfaces, are a common way for different software systems to communicate with one another. By using API connectors, low-code and no-code platforms enable users to connect their applications to external services and systems in a way that is both seamless and secure. For example, a business might need to pull data from an external CRM system, process it in their app, and display it to users. With low-code platforms, users can configure API calls to automatically retrieve this data and display it within the app, all without having to write any code. This integration capability opens up a world of possibilities for building applications that leverage data from multiple systems, whether it's for customer insights, marketing automation, or inventory management.

Another critical component of data integration in low-code and no-code platforms is data transformation. Data often comes in different formats and structures, which can make it difficult to work with across multiple systems. For example, one system may return data in JSON format, while another returns it in XML. To effectively use this data in an application, it may need to be transformed into a compatible format. Low-code and no-code platforms typically include built-in tools to handle data transformation, enabling users to map data fields, convert data types, and clean data without needing to write complex logic. These transformation tools help ensure that data from different sources is consistent and can be used together within the application, reducing the risk of errors or inconsistencies when pulling information from multiple systems.

As businesses increasingly rely on cloud-based tools and services, it is essential for low-code and no-code platforms to offer robust cloud integrations. Many platforms support integration with popular cloud services such as Amazon Web Services (AWS), Microsoft Azure, and Google Cloud, allowing users to access cloud databases, storage, and machine learning services directly from their applications. For example, a user might create an application that retrieves data from a cloud-based CRM, processes it, and then stores the results in a cloud database. With cloud integrations built into the platform, users can easily connect their applications to cloud infrastructure, ensuring that data is stored securely and can be accessed by multiple systems or users. This seamless integration between low-code/no-code applications and cloud services helps businesses scale their operations more effectively and leverage the vast array of cloud tools available.

Moreover, data security and privacy are of paramount importance when integrating data from various sources. Low-code and no-code platforms are designed with security in mind, providing built-in features to ensure that data is handled safely and in compliance with regulations. These platforms typically offer encryption, role-based access control, and user authentication features to protect sensitive data. When integrating external data, it is crucial to ensure that the data is transferred securely, especially when dealing with personally identifiable information (PII) or financial data. Many platforms also comply with industry standards and regulations, such as the General Data Protection Regulation (GDPR) in Europe or the Health Insurance Portability and Accountability Act (HIPAA) in the United States, ensuring that businesses can build compliant applications that safeguard their users' data.

Data synchronization is another important aspect of integration in low-code and no-code platforms. Many businesses use multiple systems that need to be kept in sync, whether it's updating inventory levels, synchronizing customer records, or ensuring that sales data is up-to-date across all systems. Low-code and no-code platforms often provide tools to automate data synchronization between systems, ensuring that changes in one system are reflected in others in real time. This eliminates the need for manual updates and reduces the risk of data discrepancies. Users can configure synchronization rules to specify when and how data should be updated, and the platform handles the rest, ensuring that the data remains consistent across all applications.

The ability to integrate data from various sources is what makes low-code and no-code platforms so powerful for businesses looking to create customized, data-driven applications. By providing pre-built connectors, API integrations, data transformation tools, cloud integration capabilities, and robust security features, these platforms enable users to build sophisticated applications that pull, process, and display data from multiple systems. The integration process is made accessible, fast, and efficient, empowering users to create applications that meet their specific needs without requiring complex coding or development expertise. As the demand for real-time data and interconnected systems grows, the importance of data integration in low-code and no-code platforms will continue to play a critical role in enabling businesses to innovate and thrive in an increasingly digital world.

Creating and Managing Workflows Without Writing Code

Workflows are essential in automating and optimizing business processes, ensuring that tasks are carried out in a systematic, organized manner. Traditionally, workflows were created using custom code, which required a deep understanding of programming. However, with the rise of low-code and no-code platforms, creating and managing workflows has become accessible to a broader range of users, including those with little to no coding experience. These platforms provide intuitive tools that enable users to design, automate, and manage workflows using visual interfaces, significantly reducing the complexity and time required for implementation.

In low-code and no-code environments, workflows are built through graphical interfaces that allow users to map out the steps in a process visually. These platforms often feature drag-and-drop functionality, which allows users to select and place actions or tasks in a logical sequence. This visual approach to workflow creation makes it possible for business users, who may not have any technical expertise, to design and automate workflows that meet their needs. Instead of writing lines of code to define the flow of actions, users can simply connect pre-configured elements on the platform's interface, effectively creating workflows through point-and-click interactions.

The design of workflows in these platforms often involves specifying the sequence of tasks or actions to be performed, along with the conditions under which those tasks should occur. For example, a user may want to create a workflow that triggers a series of actions when a customer submits a contact form on a website. The first step might involve sending an email to the customer, the second step could be creating a task for a sales representative to follow up, and the third step might involve updating the customer's record in a database. These actions can be connected together in a workflow, and the platform will ensure that each step occurs in the right order, without the need for any coding.

One of the key advantages of building workflows without writing code is the speed with which users can develop and deploy solutions. Traditional workflow creation in custom-coded environments often requires significant time and resources to implement. It involves writing, debugging, and testing code to ensure that the workflow functions as expected. In contrast, no-code and low-code platforms enable users to rapidly create and iterate on workflows without worrying about the technicalities of code. This allows businesses to respond more quickly to changing needs, implement new processes, and make adjustments as required. For instance, if a business identifies a need to streamline its approval process for invoices, a user could quickly design a workflow in a no-code platform that automates the routing of invoices for approval, reducing the time spent on manual tasks and speeding up the overall process.

The ability to manage workflows without writing code is particularly beneficial in terms of reducing dependency on IT teams. In many organizations, creating and managing workflows traditionally falls under the domain of technical experts, who may be bogged down with numerous other tasks. Low-code and no-code platforms empower business users to take ownership of their workflows, reducing the need for constant collaboration with IT departments. This self-sufficiency not only speeds up the development and deployment process but also allows IT teams to focus on more complex and high-priority projects. The platform's ease of use enables business users, such as marketing managers or operations directors, to create, modify, and optimize workflows that are tailored to their specific needs.

A major feature in these platforms is the inclusion of automated triggers. Triggers are conditions that automatically initiate a workflow when certain criteria are met. For instance, a user might set up a trigger that activates a workflow whenever a new lead is added to the system. Once the trigger condition is met, the platform automatically runs the series of actions that make up the workflow. These triggers can be based on a wide range of factors, including data input, time-based events, or interactions with external systems. By automating the initiation of workflows, businesses can save time, reduce human error, and ensure that tasks are completed consistently and without delay.

Moreover, low-code and no-code platforms allow users to define and manage conditional logic within workflows. Conditional logic helps to control the flow of tasks based on specific criteria. For example, if a customer's order value exceeds a certain amount, the workflow could include a step to assign the order to a senior sales representative. If the value is below that threshold, the workflow may route the order to a different representative. This ability to introduce decision points into workflows enables businesses to design more sophisticated processes that can adapt to different scenarios. Even without writing code, users can create dynamic workflows that respond to varying conditions, improving efficiency and ensuring that tasks are processed according to business rules.

Additionally, low-code and no-code platforms often include features for monitoring and optimizing workflows. These features provide real-time visibility into the performance of workflows, allowing users to track the progress of tasks and identify potential bottlenecks. Some platforms include dashboards that display key metrics, such as the number of completed tasks, pending actions, or the time taken for specific steps in the workflow. By providing these insights, users can identify areas for improvement and make data-driven decisions to optimize workflows. For example, if a workflow is taking longer than expected due to a bottleneck in a specific step, the user can analyze the workflow and make adjustments to ensure that tasks are completed more efficiently.

Integrating external systems and services into workflows is another powerful feature offered by low-code and no-code platforms. Many businesses rely on various software systems, such as customer relationship management (CRM) tools, marketing platforms, or accounting software, to manage their operations. These platforms often include pre-built connectors to these third-party services, allowing users to integrate them into their workflows with minimal effort. For example, a user could design a workflow that pulls customer data from a CRM system and sends an email to the customer using a marketing automation platform. By connecting different systems, businesses can streamline their processes, automate data exchange, and eliminate manual data entry.

Although low-code and no-code platforms enable users to create and manage workflows without writing code, they are not limited to simple applications. Many of these platforms are capable of handling complex workflows, supporting a wide range of business needs. From simple task automation to intricate multi-step processes involving external systems, these platforms provide the flexibility and power to create workflows that meet the unique requirements of different industries. Whether it is streamlining approval processes, automating lead management, or integrating customer data from multiple sources, users can design workflows that are both efficient and scalable.

Creating and managing workflows without writing code democratizes the development process, empowering users across different roles and departments to design solutions that improve business operations. By leveraging the capabilities of low-code and no-code platforms, organizations can streamline their processes, enhance collaboration between business and IT teams, and reduce the time required to bring new ideas to life. This empowerment of non-technical users not only accelerates the workflow development process but also fosters a culture of innovation, allowing businesses to continuously evolve and adapt to changing demands in the digital landscape.

Understanding and Implementing Business Logic

Business logic is a critical element in any application, as it governs the rules, calculations, and data manipulation that drive how the software operates and interacts with its users. It defines the functional behavior of an application based on the needs and requirements of the business. Business logic essentially provides the intelligence behind the application, determining what data is needed, how it should be processed, and what actions should be taken based on specific conditions or inputs. In the context of low-code and no-code development platforms, understanding and implementing business logic is crucial to creating applications that not only meet functional needs but also ensure smooth, efficient, and accurate operations within the defined business processes.

In traditional application development, business logic is implemented through complex code, often involving custom programming to handle calculations, conditional flows, and interactions with external systems. However, low-code and no-code platforms abstract much of this complexity, providing visual tools and pre-built components that allow users to define and implement business logic without writing code. These platforms use workflows, triggers, and conditions that can be configured through intuitive interfaces, making it possible for business users and non-developers to implement sophisticated logic without needing a deep understanding of programming languages.

One of the core elements of business logic in low-code and no-code platforms is the ability to define rules and conditions that dictate how data should be processed. For instance, a business logic rule might be set to automatically calculate the price of an order based on the quantity of items purchased, applying discounts or taxes as necessary. In a no-code environment, this could be done by selecting pre-built components that define the calculation steps and conditions, such as a "calculate" action or a "conditional" action based on specific data inputs. These rules can be applied to forms, workflows, or any other data-processing elements within the application, ensuring that the data is handled according to the business requirements.

The ability to define conditional logic is one of the most important aspects of implementing business logic. In any business process, different actions often need to be taken based on varying inputs or conditions. For example, in an e-commerce application, an order might need to be processed differently depending on whether the customer is a first-time buyer or a returning customer. The business logic must define these conditions, ensuring that the appropriate steps are followed for each scenario. In low-code and no-code platforms, users can configure conditions by setting up logic that triggers different actions based on the data provided. These conditions are often simple to set up, using dropdown menus and visual interfaces to define when certain actions should occur. Whether it is routing an order to a specific department, sending an email notification, or updating a database, the platform makes it possible to define these conditions without writing a single line of code.

Another key component of business logic in low-code and no-code platforms is the use of workflows. Workflows are sequences of actions or processes that are triggered automatically or manually, depending on the defined conditions. These workflows can handle a wide range of tasks, such as submitting forms, processing payments, updating databases, or generating reports. In low-code/no-code platforms, workflows are designed using visual tools that allow users to drag and drop actions and conditions into place. For example, if a user submits a contact form, the workflow could trigger an action to send an acknowledgment email, log the submission in a database, and notify a team member. By automating these tasks, workflows reduce the need for manual intervention, increase accuracy, and help ensure that processes are followed consistently across the organization.

Data integration also plays a significant role in implementing business logic. Most business applications require integration with external systems, whether it is retrieving customer data from a CRM, processing payments through a payment gateway, or updating inventory records in an ERP system. Low-code and no-code platforms simplify this process by providing pre-built connectors that allow users to link their applications to these external systems. The business logic is then designed to interact with this integrated data, allowing the application to make decisions based on real-time information. For instance, an order-processing workflow may need to check inventory levels before confirming a purchase. If the stock is unavailable, the business logic might automatically route the order to a backorder status or notify the customer of the delay. The ability to seamlessly integrate data from multiple sources and apply business logic accordingly is one of the key strengths of low-code/no-code platforms.

While no-code platforms simplify the implementation of business logic, they still require users to have a solid understanding of the logic itself. The platform might make it easy to set up triggers, actions, and conditions, but users must be able to define the underlying rules that will drive the application's behavior. This requires understanding the business requirements and translating them into the appropriate logic for the platform. For example, an accountant might need to implement business logic that calculates tax rates based on the user's location, or a marketing manager might need to set up rules to segment leads based on their engagement with marketing campaigns. While these actions are easy to configure using a no-code platform, they still require users to understand the business process they are automating and how the logic should function.

In many low-code and no-code platforms, there is also the ability to define more advanced logic using formulas or expressions. These platforms often provide users with a formula editor that allows them to create complex expressions to manipulate data or perform calculations. For example, a user might write a formula to calculate the total cost of an order by multiplying the quantity by the unit price and then applying a discount. These formulas can be combined with other components of the workflow, enabling users to implement more sophisticated logic that can handle a wide range of scenarios. While users don't need to write code to create these formulas, they still need to understand the logic behind them and how they will be applied to the data.

Error handling and validation are also critical aspects of business logic. In any application, it is essential to ensure that the data being entered is correct and consistent. Low-code and no-code platforms provide tools to define validation rules that check the input data before it is processed. For instance, a user might define a rule that requires an email field to contain a valid email address or that a date field must be filled out before submitting a form. These validation rules help ensure that errors are caught before they cause issues further down the line. Additionally, business logic can be used to handle exceptions and error messages, notifying users when something goes wrong or when the data does not meet the expected criteria.

The implementation of business logic in low-code and no-code platforms enables organizations to automate a wide range of processes, from simple tasks like sending emails to more complex workflows involving external systems and data. By using visual interfaces and pre-built components, business users can design and implement logic that fits their specific needs, making it easier to build applications that solve real-world problems without needing a deep understanding of programming. This approach democratizes application development, allowing more individuals within an organization to contribute to creating solutions that drive business efficiency and innovation. As low-code and no-code platforms continue to evolve, the ability to define and implement sophisticated business logic without writing code will remain one of their most powerful features.

Automating Processes with Low-Code/No-Code Tools

Automation is at the core of modern business operations, enabling organizations to streamline their workflows, reduce manual effort, and increase efficiency. In the past, automating business processes typically required complex coding and the involvement of skilled developers. However, with the advent of low-code and no-code platforms, businesses now have access to powerful automation tools that allow users with little to no coding knowledge to automate processes quickly and effectively. These platforms provide intuitive interfaces that simplify the creation of automation workflows, enabling organizations to automate tasks, integrate systems, and reduce the burden of manual operations.

The primary benefit of using low-code and no-code tools for automation is that they democratize the development process. Traditionally, automation required deep technical expertise and experience with programming languages, which limited its accessibility to only those who had specialized knowledge. With low-code and no-code platforms, business users, analysts, and even non-technical staff can automate processes by simply configuring pre-built components and workflows. These users can define actions, set conditions, and specify triggers through visual interfaces, significantly reducing the complexity involved in the process. As a result, employees from various departments—whether marketing, sales, operations, or customer service—can participate in automation initiatives, driving innovation across the organization.

At the heart of low-code and no-code automation tools are workflows. Workflows are a series of automated actions or tasks that are executed in response to specific triggers or conditions. These workflows can range from simple actions, such as sending an email when a form is submitted, to more complex processes that involve integrating multiple systems and performing data manipulations. In a low-code or no-code platform, users design workflows using a graphical interface that allows them to arrange these actions and conditions in a sequence. Users simply need to drag and drop different components, such as triggers, actions, and conditions, into the workflow builder, and the platform handles the underlying logic and execution. This ease of use allows businesses to automate processes that were previously too complex or resource-intensive to automate manually.

One of the key features of low-code and no-code automation tools is the ability to define triggers and actions. A trigger is an event or condition that initiates an automated workflow. For example, a user might define a trigger that activates the workflow when a new customer signs up on a website. Once the trigger is met, the platform automatically initiates a series of actions, such as sending a welcome email, creating a record in a CRM system, and adding the customer to a marketing list. The ability to define triggers based on various conditions—such as time, data input, or external events—ensures that workflows can be tailored to meet the specific needs of the business. This flexibility makes it possible to automate a wide range of tasks across different departments.

Another important aspect of automation in low-code and no-code platforms is the integration of different systems. In most organizations, multiple software tools and systems are used to manage different aspects of the business, such as customer data, sales, inventory, and marketing. Low-code and no-code platforms offer pre-built integrations that allow users to connect these systems and automate the flow of data between them. For example, a user might set up an automation workflow that synchronizes customer data between a CRM and an email marketing platform. When a new customer is added to the CRM, the platform automatically triggers an action to add that customer to a marketing campaign. By eliminating the need for manual data entry or custom integrations, low-code and no-code platforms ensure that data remains consistent across systems and that business processes are more efficient.

Automation tools in low-code and no-code platforms also support conditional logic, which allows businesses to create more sophisticated workflows. Conditional logic enables users to define specific rules for how tasks should be executed depending on the data or circumstances. For instance, an automation workflow might include a condition that checks whether a customer's order is above a certain value before offering them a discount. If the order value meets the threshold, the platform automatically applies the discount; if not, the workflow continues without making any changes. By using conditional logic, businesses can create workflows that adapt to different scenarios, ensuring that processes are executed in the right way under different conditions.

In addition to automating individual tasks, low-code and no-code platforms allow businesses to automate entire business processes. For example, a company might automate the process of onboarding new employees by setting up a workflow that sends out welcome emails, schedules training sessions, and assigns tasks to different team members as soon as an employee is hired. This automation not only saves time but also ensures that important tasks are not overlooked or forgotten. Business process automation (BPA) in low-code and no-code platforms can streamline everything from HR and finance operations to customer support and supply chain management, helping businesses run more smoothly and efficiently.

The ability to monitor and manage automated processes is another valuable feature offered by low-code and no-code tools. Many platforms include dashboards or reporting features that provide real-time insights into the performance of automated workflows. These dashboards display key metrics, such as the number of completed tasks, pending actions, or any errors that may have occurred. This visibility into the execution of automated processes helps businesses identify potential issues and optimize workflows for better performance. For example, if a workflow that processes customer orders is taking longer than expected, the business can analyze the data to pinpoint where delays are occurring and adjust the workflow accordingly. The ability to monitor automation ensures that businesses can maintain control over their processes, even when those processes are automated.

Low-code and no-code platforms also provide the flexibility to modify and adapt automated workflows as business needs change. As organizations grow and evolve, their workflows may need to be adjusted to accommodate new processes, systems, or regulatory requirements. With traditional automation methods, modifying workflows often involves extensive re-coding or the involvement of IT teams. In contrast, low-code and no-code platforms enable users to easily modify workflows by simply dragging and dropping components to make changes. This ability to quickly adjust workflows ensures that businesses can stay agile and responsive to changing conditions, without having to rely on a development team to make updates.

Security and compliance are critical considerations in any automation process, and low-code and no-code platforms are designed to address these concerns. These platforms include built-in security features, such as data encryption, role-based access controls, and user authentication, to protect sensitive data during automated processes. Additionally, many platforms offer tools to help businesses ensure compliance with industry regulations, such as GDPR or HIPAA, by enforcing data privacy and protection measures throughout the automation process.

The automation of processes using low-code and no-code tools empowers organizations to streamline operations, improve efficiency, and reduce human error. By making automation accessible to non-technical users, these platforms open up opportunities for innovation and productivity that were once reserved for IT professionals. With the ability to create, manage, and monitor workflows without writing a single line of code, businesses can take full advantage of automation to optimize their processes, improve accuracy, and ensure that operations run smoothly across departments.

Connecting Low-Code/No-Code Applications to External Systems

In today's interconnected digital landscape, the ability to integrate applications with external systems is essential for creating efficient, data-driven business solutions. Low-code and no-code platforms have revolutionized the way businesses build applications by simplifying the process of connecting to external systems, such as databases, APIs, cloud services, and other third-party applications. This functionality is particularly powerful because it allows businesses to leverage existing systems while building custom applications that can streamline workflows, automate processes, and enhance user experiences. Understanding how low-code and no-code platforms enable these connections and the methods used to achieve them is crucial for businesses that want to create flexible, scalable applications without the need for extensive coding expertise.

At the core of connecting low-code and no-code applications to external systems are APIs (Application Programming Interfaces). APIs act as intermediaries that allow one software system to communicate with another, exchanging data and triggering actions between applications. In a traditional development environment, connecting to APIs typically involves writing custom code to handle requests, manage authentication, and process the returned data. However, low-code and no-code platforms simplify this process by offering pre-built connectors and easy-to-use interfaces that allow users to integrate APIs without needing to write any code. These connectors provide a simple way to establish communication between applications, enabling businesses to pull data from external sources or send data to other systems in real-time.

One of the significant advantages of low-code and no-code platforms is their ability to integrate a wide range of third-party services and systems with minimal effort. Common integrations include cloud storage services like Google Drive or Dropbox, customer relationship management (CRM) systems like Salesforce, payment gateways such as PayPal or Stripe, and marketing platforms like Mailchimp or HubSpot. The pre-built connectors provided by these platforms enable users to connect their applications to these services seamlessly. For example, a user could create an application that automatically updates a contact record in a CRM system whenever a customer submits a form on the company's website. This integration eliminates the need for manual data entry and ensures that information is kept up-to-date across all systems.

Low-code and no-code platforms also provide functionality for connecting to databases, both on-premises and in the cloud. These platforms make it easy to interact with databases such as MySQL, PostgreSQL, Microsoft SQL Server, and cloud-based databases like Amazon RDS or Google Cloud SQL. Users can connect their applications to these databases without writing complex SQL queries or configuring database drivers manually. Instead, they can use the platform's visual interface to define the relationships between different data entities, create tables, and retrieve or update data as needed. This makes it easy to build data-driven applications that rely on external databases, such as inventory management systems, employee databases, or customer analytics platforms.

The ability to connect low-code and no-code applications to external systems extends beyond just databases and APIs. These platforms also support integrations with various business tools and services that organizations use to manage day-to-day operations. For instance, a business may need to automate the process of creating support tickets in a helpdesk system like Zendesk whenever a customer submits a complaint form. In this case, the low-code or no-code platform can connect the application to Zendesk's API, enabling the creation of tickets automatically and streamlining the customer support process. These kinds of integrations allow businesses to automate repetitive tasks, reduce manual intervention, and ensure that data flows seamlessly between applications, enhancing operational efficiency.

Another key feature of connecting low-code and no-code applications to external systems is the ability to work with webhooks. Webhooks are user-defined HTTP callbacks that allow one system to notify another system when an event occurs. For example, a business might want to receive a notification when a customer places an order on their website. By configuring a webhook, the low-code or no-code application can automatically send the order details to another system, such as an order management system, or trigger further actions, such as updating inventory or sending a confirmation email to the customer. Webhooks provide an efficient way to create real-time integrations, allowing applications to respond to events instantly and without requiring constant polling of external systems.

Low-code and no-code platforms also offer the ability to handle authentication and authorization processes when connecting to external systems. This is an important consideration when integrating with third-party services that require secure access, such as payment processors, financial systems, or CRM platforms. Most platforms provide built-in authentication mechanisms, such as OAuth or API key integration, to securely connect to these services without exposing sensitive credentials. By providing secure access and managing authentication within the platform, low-code and no-code tools reduce the complexity of integration and help ensure that data remains protected during the connection process.

Data transformation is another critical aspect of integrating external systems with low-code and no-code applications. When data is transferred between systems, it may come in different formats, such as JSON, XML, or CSV. To ensure that the data can be used correctly in the target application, it often needs to be transformed into a compatible format. Many low-code and no-code platforms include built-in data transformation tools that allow users to map data fields between different systems and convert data types. For example, a user might receive customer data from a CRM in one format and need to convert it into a format that can be used in an internal database or application. By providing these tools, low-code and no-code platforms help ensure that data is accurately transferred and processed between systems, reducing the risk of errors and data inconsistencies.

While low-code and no-code platforms make it easier to connect applications to external systems, businesses must still consider issues such as scalability, performance, and error handling when designing these integrations. As applications grow and the number of external systems increases, the complexity of managing these connections can also rise. It is important to ensure that the platform can handle large volumes of data, support multiple concurrent integrations, and provide the necessary tools for troubleshooting and monitoring. Most low-code and no-code platforms offer monitoring and logging features that allow users to track the performance of their integrations, identify issues, and make adjustments as necessary.

One of the key benefits of connecting low-code and no-code applications to external systems is the ability to create more dynamic, integrated solutions. By enabling applications to interact with existing systems and services, businesses can create end-to-end processes that streamline workflows, automate tasks, and improve overall efficiency. Whether it is pulling data from a CRM to display customer details in a user interface, synchronizing data between an inventory management system and an e-commerce platform, or triggering actions based on events in external systems, low-code and no-code platforms provide the tools necessary to build interconnected applications that deliver real-time value.

Connecting low-code and no-code applications to external systems opens up a world of possibilities for businesses looking to build flexible, scalable solutions. The integration of APIs, databases, cloud services, and webhooks allows businesses to connect their applications to virtually any external system, creating seamless workflows and automating processes. By simplifying the integration process, these platforms enable users to focus on building powerful, data-driven applications that meet their specific needs without relying on complex coding or external developers. As the demand for integrated systems continues to grow, the ability to connect applications to external services will remain a vital aspect of low-code and no-code development.

Security Considerations in Low-Code/No-Code Development

As the use of low-code and no-code development platforms continues to rise, the importance of addressing security concerns becomes even more critical. These platforms enable business users, without technical expertise, to rapidly create applications, automate processes, and integrate systems. However, this ease of use and speed also present challenges, particularly in terms of maintaining robust security practices. Securing low-code and no-code applications requires careful attention to the platform's features, user access controls, data protection measures, and compliance with regulatory standards. These considerations ensure that the applications built on these platforms are secure, reliable, and resilient to cyber threats.

One of the key security challenges in low-code and no-code development is managing user access and permissions. Since these platforms are designed to empower non-technical users to build applications, it is essential to establish clear roles and responsibilities to prevent unauthorized access to sensitive data or systems. Most low-code and no-code platforms offer role-based access control (RBAC) systems, where users can be assigned different roles with varying levels of access to the platform's features. For instance, an application builder might have full access to design and configure the application, while a user with a more limited role might only have access to view data or perform specific tasks within the application. By defining access levels and assigning roles appropriately, businesses can ensure that only authorized personnel can modify or interact with sensitive parts of the application, reducing the risk of unauthorized changes or breaches.

In addition to access control, the protection of data is another significant security concern when using low-code and no-code platforms. Applications built on these platforms often handle large volumes of sensitive information, such as customer data, financial transactions, or personal identifiers. It is essential to ensure that data is encrypted both in transit and at rest. Low-code and no-code platforms that integrate with external systems or cloud services should support secure data transfer protocols, such as HTTPS and SSL/TLS, to protect data as it moves between systems. Moreover, platforms should include robust encryption mechanisms to safeguard stored data from unauthorized access, whether it is stored locally or in the cloud. These security measures help protect sensitive information from cyberattacks, such as man-in-the-middle attacks, which could compromise the integrity and confidentiality of the data.

Another critical aspect of securing low-code and no-code applications is managing application logic and ensuring that it cannot be easily bypassed or exploited. Many low-code platforms allow users to define business logic and workflows through visual tools, which can simplify the development process but may also create security vulnerabilities if not properly configured. For instance, if a user creates a workflow that includes data validation rules, it is essential that these rules are properly enforced to prevent malicious actors from bypassing them. Failure to validate input data, for example, could allow attackers to inject harmful data, such as SQL injection, into the application, potentially compromising the entire system. It is vital that developers and users understand how to apply security measures to the business logic, such as input validation, output encoding, and secure data handling, to prevent such vulnerabilities from being introduced into the application.

Integration with external systems and third-party services is another area that requires careful attention to security. Low-code and no-code platforms often provide connectors and APIs to integrate with other software, such as customer relationship management (CRM) systems, databases, or cloud services. While these integrations can enhance the functionality of the application, they also introduce potential security risks. For example, poorly configured API integrations could expose sensitive data or allow unauthorized access to external systems. To mitigate this risk, businesses should ensure that the low-code or no-code platform supports secure authentication mechanisms, such as OAuth or API keys, to restrict access to external systems. Additionally, regular audits and monitoring of third-party integrations are essential to identify and address any security gaps that may arise over time.

Compliance with industry regulations is another important security consideration in low-code and no-code development. Many businesses are subject to strict regulatory requirements, such as the General Data Protection Regulation (GDPR) in the European Union, the Health Insurance Portability and Accountability Act (HIPAA) in the United States, or the Payment Card Industry Data Security Standard (PCI DSS). These regulations impose specific requirements for data protection, privacy, and security practices. Low-code and no-code platforms must be able to support these compliance needs by providing features like data encryption, audit logs, and user activity tracking. Additionally, platforms should offer tools that help users implement secure data handling practices, such as data anonymization and secure storage of personally identifiable information (PII). By ensuring that the platform supports compliance with these regulations, businesses can minimize the risk of legal penalties and reputational damage due to non-compliance.

As with any software development, testing is an essential part of ensuring that low-code and no-code applications are secure. While low-code platforms may reduce the need for traditional coding, they still require rigorous testing to identify potential vulnerabilities. Businesses should incorporate security testing into their development process, such as penetration testing, vulnerability scanning, and code reviews, to ensure that the application is free from security flaws. Low-code and no-code platforms may provide built-in testing features, but businesses should also consider using external tools and services to conduct comprehensive security assessments. By identifying and addressing security issues early in the development process, organizations can reduce the likelihood of vulnerabilities being exploited in production.

Another critical security consideration is the platform's ability to manage and monitor applications once they are deployed. Security does not end after the application is built; continuous monitoring and maintenance are essential to ensure that the application remains secure over time. Many low-code and no-code platforms offer monitoring features that allow businesses to track user activity, system performance, and security events. This can include tracking login attempts, monitoring for unusual behavior, and reviewing application logs for potential security incidents. Regularly updating the platform and any third-party integrations is also crucial to protect against known vulnerabilities and ensure that security patches are applied promptly. These proactive measures help maintain the integrity and security of low-code and no-code applications as they are used in production environments.

Low-code and no-code platforms offer significant advantages in terms of speed, accessibility, and ease of use, but they also come with unique security challenges. Businesses must be proactive in addressing these challenges by implementing proper access controls, securing data in transit and at rest, applying robust business logic, and ensuring compliance with industry regulations. Regular testing, monitoring, and updates are also crucial to maintaining the security of these applications. By taking a comprehensive approach to security, businesses can mitigate the risks associated with low-code and no-code development and build applications that are both functional and secure.

Testing and Debugging in Low-Code/No-Code Environments

As the use of low-code and no-code platforms continues to grow, the importance of ensuring that applications are thoroughly tested and free of errors becomes increasingly evident. While these platforms make it easier for non-technical users to build applications quickly, the process of ensuring that the application works as expected remains critical. Testing and debugging are essential steps in any software development process, and while low-code/no-code platforms simplify many aspects of development, they also require careful attention to these practices. Understanding how testing and debugging are approached within these environments is crucial for creating reliable, functional applications that meet business needs.

Testing in low-code and no-code environments can initially seem less complex compared to traditional development environments due to the visual nature of the platforms. However, this simplicity can also mask the need for rigorous testing. Many low-code and no-code tools provide pre-built components, workflows, and automation, which can create interdependencies within the application. As a result, testing should cover both individual elements of the application and how those elements work together in the broader context. This involves verifying that the user interface (UI), data handling, business logic, workflows, and integrations with external systems all function correctly in real-world scenarios. While these platforms handle a significant portion of the technical complexity, it is still necessary to ensure that all components are configured and integrated correctly.

One of the first steps in testing low-code/no-code applications is functional testing, which focuses on verifying that each feature of the application works as intended. Functional testing is especially important in environments where users can build applications by configuring pre-built components. It ensures that components such as buttons, forms, workflows, and data input fields behave as expected. For example, a form may need to capture customer information, and functional testing will confirm that the form correctly collects, processes, and stores that data in the appropriate system. In addition, testing should validate that all workflows perform the desired actions, such as triggering emails or updating databases when a user submits a form or completes a task. By thoroughly testing these core features, businesses can ensure that the application will function correctly for end-users.

Another important aspect of testing in low-code/no-code platforms is integration testing. Low-code and no-code applications often need to connect with external systems, such as databases, customer relationship management (CRM) software, or third-party services. These integrations can introduce complexity and potential points of failure, making integration testing essential. The goal of integration testing is to ensure that data flows seamlessly between the application and external systems, that API calls are successful, and that the necessary information is accurately transferred. For instance, if an application needs to retrieve customer details from an external CRM system, integration testing will verify that the data is correctly pulled into the application and that the process works as expected across different scenarios. This testing helps to identify any issues in the connections between the application and external services, ensuring that all integrations are functioning as intended.

Performance testing is another critical component of the testing process in low-code and no-code environments. While these platforms are designed to simplify development, they must still be tested for performance, especially when deployed at scale. Performance testing evaluates how well the application handles user load, how quickly it processes requests, and how efficiently it interacts with databases or external systems. For instance, if a business application is expected to handle thousands of concurrent users or process large volumes of data, it is essential to test whether the platform can scale and handle the increased load without performance degradation. Performance testing in low-code and no-code platforms may require simulating high traffic and measuring system response times to ensure that the application performs adequately under real-world conditions. This type of testing helps to ensure that the application remains responsive and reliable as usage increases.

User acceptance testing (UAT) is also a key aspect of the testing process. UAT focuses on ensuring that the application meets the needs and expectations of its end-users. Since low-code and no-code platforms enable business users to build applications themselves, it is important to involve actual users in the testing process to confirm that the application aligns with business requirements and is intuitive to use. During UAT, users can test the application in a real-world environment, providing valuable feedback about its functionality, design, and usability. This feedback is crucial for making any final adjustments before deployment and ensuring that the application is ready for broader use. Additionally, involving end-users in testing helps to identify any gaps between the initial business requirements and the final application, ensuring that the solution truly meets the organization's needs.

Debugging in low-code and no-code environments follows a slightly different process than traditional development, primarily due to the visual nature of these platforms. Debugging involves identifying and resolving issues or bugs in the application. While traditional developers rely on debugging tools such as integrated development environments (IDEs) and console logs, low-code/no-code platforms often provide more user-friendly mechanisms for debugging. These tools are often visual and intuitive, making it easier for non-technical users to track down issues. For example, many platforms provide error messages, warning notifications, or visual indicators that highlight where something has gone wrong. Users can typically click on the error or warning to get more details, and in many cases, the platform will suggest potential fixes or give instructions for resolving the issue. This approach reduces the need for advanced technical knowledge and allows users to address problems quickly.

One common debugging task in low-code/no-code platforms is troubleshooting workflows. Since workflows are often central to automating processes, it is essential that they are debugged to ensure that each step is executed correctly. If an automation is not performing as expected, users can review the sequence of actions within the workflow to identify where the problem might lie. These platforms often provide debugging tools that allow users to step through workflows step by step, observing how data flows and identifying where the process breaks down. This functionality is especially useful in identifying configuration errors or issues with logic that might prevent workflows from being executed correctly.

Another key aspect of debugging is testing the data flows within the application. Low-code/no-code platforms allow users to define how data is handled, stored, and transferred within the system. Debugging in this context involves ensuring that data is properly validated, formatted, and stored in the correct locations. For example, a form that collects user information must ensure that the data is validated before being stored in a database. If there is an issue with the data collection process, users can debug the validation rules or check the data flow to identify any discrepancies.

Once the issues have been identified and corrected, regression testing is important to ensure that the fixes do not introduce new problems into the application. This involves retesting the application to confirm that previously working features still function as expected after the changes have been made. This step helps to ensure that debugging efforts do not lead to unintended side effects, maintaining the overall integrity and functionality of the application.

Testing and debugging are integral to the success of low-code and no-code development. While these platforms provide simplified tools that enable faster development, they also require a robust approach to ensure that the applications are functional, secure, and meet the business requirements. By focusing on functional testing, integration testing, performance testing, user acceptance testing, and effective debugging practices, businesses can create reliable applications that enhance operational efficiency and user satisfaction. Although low-code and no-code platforms offer accessible development environments, maintaining a strong emphasis on testing and debugging ensures that these applications meet the high standards expected in today's digital world.

Scaling Low-Code/No-Code Applications for Business Growth

As businesses grow, the demand for scalable solutions that can handle increasing workloads, users, and data becomes more critical. Low-code and no-code platforms have provided organizations with a powerful way to rapidly develop and deploy applications without the need for extensive coding expertise. These platforms enable business users, non-developers, and even small teams to create applications quickly and cost-effectively. However, as businesses scale, the challenges of maintaining and expanding these applications while ensuring that they can continue to meet the growing demands of the organization can become complex. Understanding how to scale low-code and no-code applications is essential for businesses seeking to leverage the benefits of these platforms while ensuring that their solutions remain robust, efficient, and capable of supporting future growth.

The first aspect of scaling a low-code or no-code application is ensuring that the platform itself can handle increased demands as the business grows. These platforms are often cloud-based, which provides a level of inherent scalability, allowing applications to scale horizontally by adding resources such as additional storage, computing power, or processing capacity. Cloud infrastructure enables businesses to adjust resources dynamically, ensuring that applications can handle growing numbers of users, transactions, and data without compromising performance. Low-code and no-code platforms often offer built-in scalability features, allowing users to scale their applications seamlessly with minimal manual intervention. By leveraging cloud services such as Amazon Web Services (AWS), Microsoft Azure, or Google Cloud, these platforms can automatically scale applications to meet demand without requiring significant reconfiguration or infrastructure management.

As businesses scale, it is essential to maintain performance and ensure that the application continues to meet the demands of users and systems. Performance optimization becomes increasingly important as applications grow in size and complexity. In many cases, the scalability features of low-code and no-code platforms are designed to help businesses handle larger datasets, more complex workflows, and higher levels of traffic. However, businesses should be mindful of potential bottlenecks or areas where performance could degrade as more users or data are added. For instance, if an application processes large amounts of data in real-time, it may require additional optimization of database queries, API calls, or integrations to ensure that performance remains high even as the application scales. Platforms that support database optimization, caching mechanisms, and load balancing can help businesses address these concerns and maintain high performance as their applications grow.

Another critical consideration when scaling low-code and no-code applications is managing data effectively. As businesses expand, the volume of data generated by applications can grow exponentially. The ability to store, process, and analyze large datasets efficiently becomes increasingly important as data-driven decision-making becomes more central to business operations. Low-code and no-code platforms typically offer integration with external databases and cloud storage solutions, allowing users to scale their data storage and management capabilities. However, organizations must ensure that their applications are optimized to handle the increasing volume and complexity of data. This may involve implementing efficient data retrieval and processing techniques, optimizing data models, and ensuring that the application can handle high-throughput transactions without slowing down. Data consistency and integrity also become more challenging as applications scale, so businesses must implement proper data validation and error handling mechanisms to ensure that data remains accurate and reliable.

In addition to performance and data management, scalability in low-code and no-code applications also involves ensuring that the underlying architecture can support growing numbers of users. As businesses expand, the user base for applications often increases, and applications must be able to handle higher levels of traffic without compromising the user experience. Low-code and no-code platforms typically offer features like load balancing and traffic management to distribute user requests across multiple servers or resources, helping to prevent slowdowns or outages. However, businesses need to consider whether their platform can support the increased traffic and whether the application can scale to handle large numbers of concurrent users. Features such as user authentication, session management, and access control should be carefully designed and optimized to accommodate the growing number of users without introducing security or performance issues.

One of the strengths of low-code and no-code platforms is their ability to integrate with other business systems, such as enterprise resource planning (ERP), customer relationship management (CRM), and human resources (HR) systems. As businesses scale, the need for seamless integration between applications and other internal systems becomes even more crucial. The ability to automate processes, synchronize data, and ensure that applications work in harmony with other business tools is essential for maintaining efficiency as the organization grows. Low-code and no-code platforms make it easier to connect to third-party systems and integrate data across multiple platforms, allowing businesses to expand their applications and functionality without extensive custom development. However, businesses must ensure that their integrations are scalable and able to handle increased data volumes and transaction frequencies as the business grows.

Automation is another key factor in scaling low-code and no-code applications. As businesses expand, the need for automation increases to reduce manual effort, eliminate errors, and ensure consistency across operations. Low-code and no-code platforms offer powerful automation capabilities, such as workflow automation and business rule execution, that allow businesses to streamline repetitive tasks, automate complex processes, and improve operational efficiency. These workflows can be designed to scale as the business grows, ensuring that processes remain efficient and reliable regardless of the volume of tasks. However, businesses should also consider how their automated workflows will perform under high demand and whether additional logic or optimization is required to ensure that automation scales effectively.

Governance and compliance also play an important role when scaling low-code and no-code applications. As organizations grow, they are often subject to more stringent regulatory requirements and industry standards. Ensuring that applications meet these standards while scaling can be challenging, particularly when dealing with sensitive data or operating in regulated industries such as healthcare, finance, or retail. Low-code and no-code platforms typically provide tools for managing governance, including features for audit logging, access control, and data protection. As businesses scale, it is essential to ensure that these features are properly configured to support the organization's compliance requirements. Additionally, businesses must be vigilant about maintaining security best practices, such as secure data storage, encryption, and secure user authentication, to protect both the application and the data it handles.

Maintaining flexibility and adaptability is another important consideration when scaling low-code and no-code applications. As business needs evolve and technology changes, applications must be able to adapt to new requirements. One of the benefits of low-code and no-code platforms is that they provide a high degree of flexibility, allowing users to modify applications quickly and easily without relying on a development team. However, as applications scale, it is essential to ensure that the platform can continue to accommodate new features, integrations, and customizations. Businesses should choose low-code and no-code platforms that provide a range of customization options and the ability to scale up or down as needed.

Scalability in low-code and no-code environments is about much more than just adding resources or accommodating more users. It involves building applications that can handle increased complexity, larger datasets, and more integrations while maintaining performance and security. By leveraging the scalability features of these platforms, businesses can create applications that grow with them, ensuring that their technology can support the demands of a larger organization. Whether through cloud infrastructure, automated workflows, optimized data management, or seamless integrations, businesses can scale their low-code and no-code applications effectively to meet the demands of an expanding organization. As businesses continue to grow, understanding how to scale applications on low-code and no-code platforms will be critical to staying competitive and maintaining operational efficiency.

Managing Application Lifecycle with Low-Code/No-Code Platforms

Managing the lifecycle of an application is a critical component of ensuring its success, especially as businesses increasingly rely on technology to drive operations and innovation. The traditional application development lifecycle involves stages such as planning, design, development, testing, deployment, maintenance, and retirement. While low-code and no-code platforms significantly simplify the development and deployment of applications, they still require a comprehensive approach to lifecycle management. These platforms provide businesses with tools that help manage applications from initial conception through ongoing maintenance and updates. Understanding how to manage the application lifecycle in low-code and no-code environments is crucial for organizations that aim to scale their operations and continuously improve their applications over time.

The first stage in managing the application lifecycle with low-code and no-code platforms is planning. The planning phase remains as important in low-code and no-code environments as it is in traditional software development. Although these platforms allow for rapid prototyping and development, organizations must still define the scope, goals, and requirements for the application to ensure that it meets the business's needs. Planning involves identifying the stakeholders, understanding the processes that need to be automated or improved, and setting clear objectives for the application. With low-code and no-code platforms, this stage is often more collaborative because business users can directly contribute to the planning process without needing technical expertise. By involving non-developers early on, organizations can ensure that the application is aligned with business needs and that the correct features are prioritized.

Once planning is complete, the next phase in the application lifecycle is design. Low-code and no-code platforms simplify this stage by providing visual interfaces that allow users to design the application's user interface (UI) and workflows. Since these platforms often come with pre-built components, templates, and drag-and-drop functionality, users can focus on the structure, appearance, and user experience of the application without getting bogged down in coding. The design phase is crucial because it directly impacts how users will interact with the application. A well-designed application will not only meet business requirements but also provide a seamless and intuitive user experience. Low-code and no-code platforms make it easier for users to iterate on designs quickly, allowing businesses to refine the user interface and workflows based on feedback from stakeholders or initial testing.

Development in low-code and no-code platforms is often more streamlined than in traditional development environments due to the simplified coding requirements. These platforms abstract much of the underlying complexity of software development, allowing users to create applications by configuring pre-built components and defining workflows rather than writing custom code. While this speeds up the development process, it is important to maintain a focus on creating an application that is scalable, secure, and capable of meeting the organization's long-term needs. Even though users do not need to write code to create the functionality of the application, they must still define business logic, integrate external systems, and ensure that the application performs as expected. Low-code and no-code platforms provide visual tools for creating workflows and automating processes, and these tools must be configured correctly to avoid errors or issues down the line.

Testing is an essential stage in the application lifecycle, regardless of the development method used. Low-code and no-code platforms provide several tools for testing applications before they are deployed to production. Testing in these platforms generally involves functional testing to ensure that the application works as intended, integration testing to verify that the application communicates effectively with external systems, and performance testing to ensure that the application can handle the expected user load. Since low-code and no-code applications are built with pre-configured components, much of the testing process involves ensuring that these components are correctly integrated and configured. Visual interfaces in these platforms also make it easier to track issues, as developers and non-technical users alike can quickly identify and troubleshoot errors. By thoroughly testing the application in various scenarios, businesses can minimize the risk of bugs or failures when the application is deployed to users.

Deployment is another critical stage of the application lifecycle, and low-code and no-code platforms offer significant advantages in this area. Traditional application deployment often involves configuring servers, managing databases, and setting up cloud services, all of which require extensive technical expertise. However, low-code and no-code platforms typically handle much of this complexity for users. These platforms allow users to deploy applications to cloud environments or on-premises servers with minimal manual intervention. The process is often as simple as clicking a button or selecting deployment options through the platform's interface. This simplifies the deployment process, allowing businesses to release applications more quickly and at a lower cost. Additionally, many low-code and no-code platforms provide automatic updates, ensuring that any changes made to the application are reflected in real-time without requiring extensive downtime.

After deployment, the next phase of the application lifecycle is maintenance. Even though low-code and no-code platforms simplify the development and deployment process, applications still require ongoing maintenance to ensure that they remain secure, functional, and aligned with changing business needs. Maintenance tasks can include bug fixes, performance optimization, updates to workflows, and security patches. Low-code and no-code platforms typically offer easy-to-use tools for managing these updates, such as a visual interface for modifying workflows, integrating new systems, or updating business logic. The ability to make changes without needing to write code ensures that businesses can quickly adapt their applications in response to new requirements or issues, improving the agility of the organization.

Security is a critical consideration during both the development and maintenance phases of the application lifecycle. Low-code and no-code platforms often provide built-in security features, such as role-based access control, data encryption, and authentication mechanisms. These features help ensure that the application remains secure as it evolves and that access to sensitive data is properly managed. Additionally, businesses must stay vigilant about maintaining security best practices throughout the lifecycle, particularly as new vulnerabilities are discovered or as the application is integrated with additional systems. Regular security audits, monitoring, and updates are necessary to maintain the integrity and safety of low-code and no-code applications.

As businesses continue to scale and evolve, their applications will need to grow and adapt. Low-code and no-code platforms allow for continuous improvement of applications through iterative updates, but organizations must also consider the long-term scalability of their solutions. As more users interact with the application or as more data is processed, the platform must be able to handle these increased demands without compromising performance. This might involve optimizing workflows, improving data management strategies, or integrating with additional systems to handle larger datasets. Low-code and no-code platforms often provide the tools to manage these changes efficiently, allowing businesses to scale their applications without needing to completely rebuild them.

Managing the application lifecycle with low-code and no-code platforms offers businesses a streamlined, flexible approach to creating and maintaining applications. These platforms simplify many of the traditional challenges of software development, such as coding, testing, and deployment, while still allowing for customization and scalability. By taking a systematic approach to planning, designing, developing, testing, deploying, maintaining, and securing low-code and no-code applications, businesses can ensure that their applications continue to meet their needs and grow with their organization. The agility and speed offered by these platforms allow businesses to adapt to changing market conditions, enhance operational efficiency, and provide innovative solutions to their users. Managing the application lifecycle effectively ensures that low-code and no-code applications remain functional, secure, and aligned with the organization's goals throughout their entire lifespan.

Collaboration Between Developers and Business Users

Collaboration between developers and business users has always been an essential part of software development, but with the rise of low-code and no-code platforms, this collaboration has taken on new dimensions. These platforms have bridged the gap between business users, who have a deep understanding of the organization's needs and goals, and developers, who possess the technical expertise to build and optimize applications. By providing a more intuitive and accessible development environment, low-code and no-code platforms empower both technical and non-technical stakeholders to work together more effectively, improving the speed, quality, and relevance of the applications created. The dynamics of this collaboration, however, require a shift in mindset, communication, and workflow practices to ensure success.

In traditional development environments, the divide between developers and business users was often significant. Developers worked largely in isolation, translating business requirements into technical specifications and code, while business users, often distanced from the development process, could only provide limited input or feedback. This separation led to a number of challenges, including miscommunications, delays, and applications that were not fully aligned with business needs. Low-code and no-code platforms have dramatically changed this dynamic by allowing business users to participate directly in the creation and iteration of applications. These platforms enable users to build, test, and modify applications with little to no coding knowledge, making them an integral part of the development process from start to finish.

The involvement of business users in the application development process allows for a more agile approach to software creation. Traditionally, business requirements were often captured at the beginning of a project and then handed off to developers to execute. This linear process could result in a product that did not fully meet the needs of the business, as there was limited opportunity for feedback during the development phase. With low-code and no-code platforms, business users can build prototypes and test features as they go, providing valuable feedback that can be used to refine and improve the application in real-time. This iterative approach ensures that the application is better aligned with the evolving needs of the business, reducing the risk of costly changes or delays later in the project.

Moreover, low-code and no-code platforms encourage more frequent communication between business users and developers. While business users are empowered to create and modify applications, developers remain essential in overseeing more complex integrations, ensuring that security measures are in place, and addressing any technical limitations or challenges that arise. Developers can work alongside business users to ensure that the application meets both functional and technical requirements, offering guidance when necessary. In this collaborative environment, developers are no longer isolated in their coding tasks, but rather play a key role in enabling business users to bring their ideas to life while also ensuring that the application's technical integrity is maintained.

This shift toward collaboration requires both business users and developers to embrace new roles and ways of working. Business users must be willing to step out of their traditional roles and engage more directly with the technical aspects of application development. While low-code and no-code platforms reduce the complexity of development, business users still need to understand the basic principles of application design, user experience, and data flow. As they take on more responsibility in the development process, they must also learn to work closely with developers to ensure that their vision is translated effectively into the application. This requires an open and collaborative mindset, where feedback is shared freely, and both parties are willing to learn from each other.

On the other hand, developers must be ready to act as facilitators and mentors rather than as sole creators. While they continue to handle more complex tasks, such as custom integrations, database management, and security, developers must also provide guidance to business users on best practices for application design and development. This collaborative dynamic requires developers to communicate more clearly with non-technical stakeholders, translating technical concepts into language that business users can understand. This shift not only fosters better collaboration but also helps to ensure that business users can effectively utilize the tools provided by low-code and no-code platforms.

For businesses to fully leverage the benefits of low-code and no-code platforms, they must create an environment that encourages this type of collaboration. This includes fostering a culture of open communication and mutual respect between business users and developers. Clear processes should be established for how feedback will be collected, addressed, and incorporated into the development cycle. Regular meetings, feedback loops, and testing sessions can help ensure that all stakeholders are aligned and that the application meets business needs. Additionally, businesses should provide training and resources to ensure that business users are equipped to work effectively within the low-code or no-code platform. This may include providing access to tutorials, guides, and support from technical teams, helping users to become more comfortable with the platform and its capabilities.

One of the key advantages of improved collaboration between business users and developers is the ability to reduce the backlog of IT projects. Traditionally, the IT department has been responsible for managing all aspects of application development, leading to long wait times for new features or improvements. Low-code and no-code platforms enable business users to take ownership of certain aspects of application development, which can help alleviate pressure on IT departments and free up developers to focus on more complex or strategic initiatives. This improved efficiency leads to faster delivery of applications and features, allowing businesses to respond more quickly to changing market demands or new business opportunities.

Another benefit of this collaboration is the alignment of business objectives with application development. With business users involved in the development process, applications are more likely to meet the specific needs and goals of the organization. Developers can work alongside business stakeholders to ensure that the application is designed to optimize processes, improve customer experiences, and achieve key business outcomes. This close collaboration ensures that applications are not just functional but are aligned with the broader strategic objectives of the organization, ultimately driving better business results.

In many cases, low-code and no-code platforms also allow for the integration of various business systems, enabling developers and business users to collaborate on building applications that interact with multiple systems. These integrations can streamline workflows and automate tasks across different platforms, improving efficiency and reducing the risk of errors. Business users can play an active role in defining how these integrations should work, ensuring that the data flows smoothly between systems and that the application meets business requirements.

Collaboration between developers and business users is key to the success of low-code and no-code development initiatives. These platforms have made it possible for non-technical users to engage in the development process, providing valuable insights and feedback that help shape the final product. By fostering open communication, mutual understanding, and shared responsibility, businesses can create applications that are more closely aligned with their needs, more responsive to market changes, and more efficient to develop and deploy. This collaboration helps ensure that applications are not only technically sound but also truly meet the business needs, driving innovation and improving overall business performance.

Governance and Compliance in Low-Code/No-Code Development

Low-code and no-code platforms have significantly changed the landscape of application development by democratizing the process, making it accessible to non-technical users while also accelerating the creation and deployment of applications. However, as organizations increasingly use these platforms to develop business-critical applications, concerns about governance and compliance have become paramount. Governance refers to the processes, policies, and controls that ensure the applications being developed are aligned with the organization's objectives, security standards, and industry regulations. Compliance, on the other hand, involves adhering to legal, regulatory, and internal standards, particularly around data protection, privacy, and security. Managing governance and ensuring compliance in low-code and no-code environments require careful planning, the right tools, and a strategic approach to mitigate risks while maximizing the benefits of these platforms.

One of the most significant challenges in low-code and no-code development environments is ensuring that governance practices are effectively implemented. These platforms empower business users, including marketers, analysts, and department managers, to build applications without relying heavily on IT departments. While this accessibility speeds up application delivery, it can also lead to a lack of oversight, making it difficult to enforce standardized governance practices. Applications developed by various business units can end up lacking consistency, security, and alignment with overall business objectives, especially if those applications are not subject to a central governance framework.

Effective governance in low-code and no-code development starts with defining clear policies that align with the organization's strategic goals and regulatory requirements. These policies should cover a range of areas, including data handling, security standards, access controls, and user permissions. Low-code and no-code platforms generally provide a range of governance tools to help manage these policies. For example, role-based access control (RBAC) allows organizations to set permissions for different types of users based on their roles within the organization. This ensures that only authorized individuals can modify critical applications, sensitive data, or key configurations. By enforcing these controls, businesses can prevent unauthorized access, ensure accountability, and maintain the integrity of the applications being developed.

In addition to access controls, another key component of governance is version control. Low-code and no-code platforms often allow users to track changes, roll back updates, and manage application versions. This is particularly important as multiple people across the organization may be involved in the development and maintenance of applications. With proper version control, organizations can ensure that changes are documented, that updates can be reviewed for compliance purposes, and that earlier versions of an application can be restored if issues arise. This level of tracking also enhances transparency, allowing businesses to have full visibility into who made changes, when those changes occurred, and what was altered. Such practices reduce the risks associated with application errors or unauthorized modifications, helping to maintain a consistent and compliant development environment.

Compliance is another crucial concern in low-code and no-code development, particularly for industries that are heavily regulated, such as healthcare, finance, and e-commerce. Organizations in these sectors must comply with strict regulations related to data protection, privacy, and security. These regulations include laws like the General Data Protection Regulation (GDPR) in the European Union, the Health Insurance Portability and Accountability Act (HIPAA) in the United States, and the Payment Card Industry Data Security Standard (PCI DSS) for organizations handling payment data. Compliance ensures that businesses meet legal obligations and protect sensitive information from breaches, which could result in significant fines and reputational damage.

Low-code and no-code platforms can support compliance efforts by providing built-in tools that facilitate secure data management, encryption, and user authentication. These platforms often come with features like data encryption both in transit and at rest, ensuring that sensitive data is protected while being transferred across networks or stored in databases. Additionally, many platforms provide authentication mechanisms such as multi-factor authentication (MFA) and single sign-on (SSO) to secure user access and minimize the risk of unauthorized data access. By implementing these security measures, businesses can ensure that their low-code and no-code applications are compliant with data privacy and security regulations.

Another important aspect of compliance is ensuring that applications adhere to internal policies around data retention, deletion, and access. In industries where regulatory requirements mandate the storage and protection of data for specific periods, low-code and no-code platforms can help automate and enforce these policies. For example, automated data retention policies can be built into the application's workflow to ensure that data is archived or deleted according to legal requirements. This reduces the risk of non-compliance and ensures that businesses are not inadvertently violating regulations due to poor data management practices.

To help enforce governance and compliance, organizations must also prioritize training and education for the users building and managing low-code/no-code applications. While these platforms are designed to be user-friendly, it is still important that employees understand the implications of data protection laws, security protocols, and organizational policies when developing applications. Providing training on the proper use of governance features, security controls, and compliance requirements is essential to ensure that applications meet the necessary standards from the outset. Organizations that neglect this training risk developing applications that may inadvertently breach regulatory requirements or expose sensitive information to potential threats.

Auditing is a critical part of governance and compliance. Regular audits of applications and development activities help organizations assess whether their low-code and no-code applications are compliant with internal and external regulations. These audits can be performed manually or through automated tools that track user activity, changes made to applications, and compliance with established policies. Auditing helps organizations identify potential vulnerabilities or gaps in their governance framework, enabling them to take corrective actions before issues arise. Additionally, audit logs provide an essential trail of documentation, which is important for meeting regulatory requirements and demonstrating compliance during inspections or investigations.

Managing risk is another important aspect of governance in low-code and no-code environments. While these platforms offer many advantages in terms of speed and accessibility, they also introduce certain risks, especially when it comes to data security and compliance. For example, the rapid development of applications can lead to the creation of shadow IT systems—applications built outside of the purview of the IT department—that may not adhere to corporate security standards. To mitigate this risk, organizations should establish clear guidelines for which platforms and applications are allowed and enforce policies that require all applications to be developed within the governance framework. This helps ensure that applications developed in low-code/no-code environments are subject to the same scrutiny and security checks as traditional applications.

Finally, it is essential for organizations to continually evaluate and improve their governance and compliance practices in low-code/no-code development. As the regulatory landscape evolves, new security threats emerge, and the platform capabilities themselves improve, businesses must remain vigilant. Regularly updating governance policies, security protocols, and compliance checks ensures that applications continue to meet evolving standards. This iterative process helps businesses stay ahead of potential risks and ensures that their low-code and no-code applications continue to operate securely and in full compliance with relevant laws.

Governance and compliance are critical to the success and sustainability of low-code and no-code applications. While these platforms empower non-technical users to develop applications quickly, they also require careful attention to security, regulatory requirements, and data management practices. By implementing clear governance frameworks, leveraging built-in compliance tools, and providing ongoing training and audits, businesses can ensure that their low-code and no-code applications are secure, compliant, and aligned with their strategic goals. Proper governance and compliance practices not only protect the business but also contribute to the long-term success of applications in an increasingly complex and regulated digital world.

Building Customizable User Interfaces with Low-Code/No-Code Tools

User interface (UI) design is one of the most critical aspects of any application, as it determines how users interact with the system. A well-designed interface enhances usability, ensures smooth user experiences, and improves the overall functionality of the application. Traditionally, creating customizable and dynamic UIs required skilled designers and developers with expertise in front-end development technologies such as HTML, CSS, and JavaScript. However, with the advent of low-code and no-code platforms, the process of building customizable user interfaces has become more accessible, even to those with little to no technical background. These platforms empower business users, designers, and even non-technical staff to create and customize user interfaces quickly and efficiently, without needing to write extensive code.

Low-code and no-code tools provide a visual interface for designing UIs, allowing users to drag and drop pre-built components to create layouts and add functionality. These platforms often come with a wide range of customizable components such as buttons, text fields, dropdown menus, and form elements that can be easily incorporated into the interface. Users can choose from a variety of templates that serve as starting points, reducing the need for designing from scratch. These templates are typically designed to address common use cases, such as login pages, contact forms, or dashboards, enabling users to quickly build applications that align with their business needs. By using these templates, businesses can significantly speed up the development process while still maintaining flexibility and control over the design.

One of the key features of low-code and no-code platforms is the ability to customize the appearance and behavior of UI components without writing any code. These platforms often offer an intuitive interface that allows users to change the properties of elements, such as size, color, font, and positioning, using simple point-and-click actions. For instance, users can adjust the background color of a button, change its text, or modify the layout of a form by dragging elements into different positions on the page. This level of customization ensures that the UI aligns with the company's branding, design guidelines, and the specific needs of the users. While these visual design tools are user-friendly, they still allow for a significant degree of customization, ensuring that applications can be tailored to meet the unique requirements of the business.

The ability to create responsive UIs is another critical aspect of building customizable user interfaces with low-code and no-code tools. In today's digital landscape, applications must be accessible across a wide range of devices, from desktop computers to mobile phones and tablets. Low-code and no-code platforms typically provide responsive design features that automatically adjust the layout of the user interface based on the size and orientation of the screen. This allows users to build applications that are optimized for different devices without needing to manually adjust the layout for each screen size. Responsive design is essential for ensuring a consistent and high-quality user experience across all devices, as it prevents elements from becoming misaligned or difficult to navigate on smaller screens. Users can customize how the interface behaves on different devices, such as adjusting font sizes or hiding certain elements on mobile screens, to enhance usability and performance.

Beyond basic design and customization, low-code and no-code platforms also enable the creation of dynamic user interfaces that respond to user input or external data. For example, users can create forms that change based on the information entered by the user, display different content depending on user roles, or update the interface in real-time based on data from external systems. This dynamic behavior is typically achieved through visual workflows and triggers that automatically adjust the interface in response to specific actions. For instance, if a user selects an option from a dropdown menu, the form could display additional fields based on that selection. Similarly, if the user inputs certain data, the system could validate the input in real-time and provide immediate feedback on whether the information is correct. These dynamic UIs not only make applications more interactive but also improve the user experience by ensuring that the interface adapts to the needs of the user as they navigate through the application.

One of the advantages of low-code and no-code platforms is that they often support integration with external data sources, allowing users to create UIs that pull and display data in real-time. For example, a business might want to display customer information, inventory levels, or sales data directly on the application's user interface. Low-code and no-code platforms make it easy to integrate data from external systems such as databases, cloud storage, or third-party services through pre-built connectors or API integrations. Users can then customize how this data is presented on the UI, choosing from various data visualization components such as tables, charts, or graphs. This integration ensures that the application's UI is always up to date with the latest data, improving decision-making and providing users with the most relevant information at all times.

In addition to integrating external data, low-code and no-code platforms often support the integration of third-party tools and services, allowing users to extend the functionality of the user interface. For example, a business might want to incorporate a payment gateway, such as PayPal or Stripe, into their application's checkout process. These platforms provide pre-configured components that enable users to integrate these services seamlessly into the UI without needing to write any code. Users can then customize how these external services are presented on the interface, such as adding payment forms, custom branding, or transaction tracking. This ability to integrate third-party services into the UI expands the capabilities of low-code and no-code applications, enabling businesses to create more comprehensive and feature-rich applications.

While low-code and no-code platforms provide a high degree of customization, there are still limitations to consider. More complex design elements or advanced interactions may require custom code. For example, if a business requires a highly customized user interface with specific animations, transitions, or interactions that go beyond the capabilities of the platform's pre-built components, writing code may still be necessary. Fortunately, many low-code and no-code platforms offer the option to insert custom code when needed, allowing developers to extend the platform's functionality while still benefiting from the simplicity and speed of the low-code/no-code environment. This hybrid approach ensures that businesses can achieve their desired level of customization while still maintaining the efficiency of low-code development.

Security is another important consideration when building customizable UIs with low-code and no-code tools. Since these applications often involve sensitive data, it is essential to implement robust security measures to protect both the users and the business. Many low-code and no-code platforms provide built-in security features such as user authentication, role-based access control, and data encryption. Users can configure these features through the platform's interface to ensure that only authorized individuals have access to certain parts of the application. These security tools help to safeguard the user interface and the data it handles, ensuring that the application complies with organizational and regulatory security requirements.

Building customizable user interfaces with low-code and no-code platforms enables organizations to create applications that are tailored to their specific business needs without requiring extensive development resources. By providing a user-friendly, visual interface for designing UIs, these platforms allow non-technical users to participate in the development process while still offering the flexibility needed to meet complex requirements. Whether designing static pages or dynamic, data-driven interfaces, low-code and no-code tools empower businesses to create engaging, functional, and responsive user interfaces that enhance the user experience and improve business outcomes.

Exploring Advanced Features of Low-Code/No-Code Platforms

Low-code and no-code platforms have dramatically transformed how applications are developed, enabling non-technical users to create robust applications with minimal coding skills. These platforms provide an array of tools that streamline the development process and lower the barrier to entry for building custom software solutions. While many people are familiar with the basic functionalities of low-code/no-code platforms, such as drag-and-drop interfaces and pre-built templates, these platforms also offer advanced features that can significantly enhance the flexibility, scalability, and complexity of applications. Exploring these advanced features is crucial for businesses that want to fully leverage the potential of these platforms to meet their unique needs.

One of the advanced features of low-code and no-code platforms is the ability to integrate with various third-party services and external systems. While most basic applications rely on internal data and workflows, many organizations need their applications to communicate with other software tools, databases, or services. For example, businesses may want to integrate their low-code or no-code applications with Customer Relationship Management (CRM) systems, Enterprise Resource Planning (ERP) systems, or marketing automation platforms. These platforms offer pre-built connectors and API integration tools that allow users to seamlessly link their applications with these external systems. With these integrations, low-code and no-code platforms can act as bridges, pulling data from one system and pushing it to another, all while ensuring that the data remains synchronized across various systems. This ability to integrate multiple systems makes these platforms powerful tools for creating data-driven applications that can streamline operations, automate tasks, and provide more insightful business intelligence.

In addition to integrations, low-code and no-code platforms also enable businesses to implement complex workflows. These workflows allow users to automate business processes, from simple tasks like sending emails to more intricate processes such as order approval, customer onboarding, or inventory management. Advanced workflow automation tools often include the ability to create multi-step processes that incorporate logic, conditional branches, and decision points. For example, a workflow might automatically trigger different actions depending on whether a form submission is from a new customer or a returning one. These workflows can be configured using a visual interface, where users can drag and drop actions and set conditions based on real-time data. This feature is especially valuable for businesses that need to automate repetitive tasks, reduce manual intervention, and ensure consistency in their operations.

Another advanced feature is the ability to customize business logic within low-code/no-code applications. While basic logic can often be handled using pre-configured templates and simple automation tools, more complex business rules may require custom logic. Low-code and no-code platforms allow users to write custom code in specific modules or components, providing greater flexibility in how the application behaves. For instance, a business might need to implement a custom pricing formula for a product based on various variables, such as the customer's purchase history, geographic location, or membership tier. By leveraging the platform's advanced logic features, users can define these custom rules using an intuitive interface that blends visual configuration with minimal code. This hybrid approach enables businesses to tailor applications to their exact needs without sacrificing the simplicity and speed of low-code/no-code development.

Data management and manipulation is another area where advanced features shine in low-code and no-code platforms. As businesses increasingly rely on data to drive decisions and optimize operations, having robust tools for handling and analyzing that data is essential. Many low-code/no-code platforms offer advanced data handling capabilities that allow users to create, manipulate, and visualize data without relying on complex database queries or coding. These tools typically include data connectors that allow users to import data from external sources, as well as powerful features for transforming, filtering, and aggregating that data within the platform. Users can build dynamic reports, dashboards, and data visualizations that provide real-time insights into key business metrics, such as sales performance, customer behavior, or inventory levels. These advanced data capabilities make it easier for businesses to turn raw data into actionable insights and make informed decisions.

Advanced security features are also an important aspect of low-code and no-code platforms, particularly for businesses that need to ensure their applications comply with strict regulatory and security standards. While low-code/no-code platforms are designed to make development faster and easier, they also need to provide robust security mechanisms to protect sensitive data and maintain application integrity. Many of these platforms include features like role-based access control (RBAC), where users can define different levels of access based on their role within the organization. For example, a marketing manager might have access to certain features of the application, while a system administrator might have full access to all configurations and settings. Other advanced security features include encryption, both for data in transit and at rest, as well as support for industry-standard authentication protocols, such as Single Sign-On (SSO) and Multi-Factor Authentication (MFA). These advanced security features are essential for ensuring that applications built on low-code/no-code platforms are both secure and compliant with data privacy regulations, such as GDPR or HIPAA.

Another powerful feature of advanced low-code and no-code platforms is the ability to deploy applications across multiple environments. As businesses scale, they often need to deploy applications in different environments, such as development, staging, and production, to test changes before they are rolled out to end-users. Many low-code/no-code platforms provide seamless deployment tools that allow businesses to quickly deploy applications across various environments with minimal manual intervention. These platforms may offer version control, automated testing, and rollback capabilities to ensure that deployments are smooth and that issues can be quickly addressed. Additionally, businesses can leverage cloud-native deployments to ensure scalability and high availability of their applications, particularly as user demand grows.

Mobile application development is another area where low-code/no-code platforms offer advanced capabilities. Many businesses require mobile apps to provide better access to their services or products for users on the go. While traditional mobile development can be complex and time-consuming, low-code/no-code platforms often provide tools for building mobile applications without requiring specialized knowledge of mobile development frameworks. These platforms offer templates, responsive design options, and drag-and-drop components that can help users create mobile apps that are fully functional and optimized for a variety of mobile devices. In many cases, these platforms also enable the integration of device-specific features, such as location services, push notifications, or camera access, allowing businesses to build fully-featured mobile applications quickly and efficiently.

Finally, many low-code/no-code platforms offer the ability to scale applications and ensure their performance as user numbers and data volumes increase. Advanced performance monitoring tools help businesses track the application's performance and identify bottlenecks or areas that need improvement. These platforms often integrate with cloud infrastructure, which can dynamically allocate resources to handle increased traffic or more complex workflows. By leveraging the scalability of cloud services, low-code/no-code platforms allow businesses to build applications that can grow and adapt to the changing needs of the organization, without the need for extensive rework or technical interventions.

Advanced features in low-code and no-code platforms empower businesses to create complex, scalable, and secure applications while still benefiting from the speed and ease of use that these platforms are known for. The ability to integrate external systems, customize business logic, manage data efficiently, and maintain high security standards allows businesses to tackle a wide range of application development needs. As these platforms evolve, they continue to offer more powerful tools that enable organizations to innovate faster, streamline operations, and meet the increasing demands of the digital world.

Deploying Low-Code/No-Code Applications

Deploying applications built on low-code and no-code platforms has become a fundamental aspect of modern business operations. These platforms allow users to create and deploy applications quickly, reducing the time from concept to production. While the development process itself is simplified through the use of intuitive interfaces, deploying these applications successfully requires careful planning, proper configuration, and an understanding of the deployment environments. Successful deployment ensures that the application runs smoothly, remains secure, and can scale as needed. Understanding the deployment process in low-code/no-code platforms is critical for businesses looking to make the most of these tools and ensure their applications are functional and reliable.

The first step in deploying a low-code or no-code application is selecting the appropriate deployment environment. Many low-code and no-code platforms offer cloud-based deployment options, which are ideal for scalability and flexibility. Cloud deployment allows businesses to deploy applications without the need for dedicated hardware or complex infrastructure management. The platform typically handles server provisioning, network configuration, and scaling automatically, making it easier for businesses to deploy applications without requiring deep IT expertise. In some cases, organizations may opt to deploy their applications on-premises if they need more control over their environment or if they have specific security or compliance requirements. Regardless of the chosen environment, it is important to ensure that the application is deployed in a secure and reliable environment to avoid performance issues and data breaches.

After selecting the deployment environment, businesses need to ensure that their low-code/no-code application is configured correctly for deployment. These platforms often come with built-in tools for managing different environments, such as development, staging, and production. For instance, developers and business users can work in a development environment, test new features in a staging environment, and deploy the application to production once everything is ready. This approach helps ensure that any issues or bugs are identified and addressed before the application is made available to end-users. Managing multiple environments is critical for maintaining a smooth deployment process, as it allows teams to perform quality checks and verify that the application works as expected under different conditions.

Before the actual deployment, thorough testing is essential. Low-code and no-code platforms typically provide tools for both functional and performance testing. Functional testing ensures that all features of the application work as expected, while performance testing evaluates how well the application handles increased loads, traffic, or data. Testing the application in a staging environment mimics real-world scenarios and helps identify any bottlenecks, errors, or inefficiencies that could affect the user experience. Ensuring that the application performs well and meets business requirements is key to avoiding costly disruptions after deployment. In addition to these tests, security testing is another crucial step to ensure the application is resistant to vulnerabilities and data breaches.

Once the application passes testing, the next step in deployment is the actual launch. Low-code and no-code platforms make this process relatively straightforward, as users can deploy applications with just a few clicks. The platform often automates many aspects of the deployment process, such as provisioning servers, setting up databases, and ensuring proper configuration of application settings. For cloud deployments, platforms may integrate with cloud providers such as Amazon Web Services (AWS), Microsoft Azure, or Google Cloud, enabling businesses to leverage the scalability and infrastructure provided by these services. This automatic provisioning makes it much easier for businesses to deploy applications rapidly without needing in-depth knowledge of cloud infrastructure management.

However, while the deployment process itself may be simple, the post-deployment phase requires ongoing monitoring and maintenance to ensure that the application continues to run smoothly. Low-code and no-code platforms often offer monitoring tools that track the performance of deployed applications. These tools provide insights into key metrics such as application uptime, response times, user activity, and system resource usage. By keeping an eye on these metrics, businesses can detect and address any issues before they impact users. For example, if a particular feature is slowing down the application or if the server load is too high, businesses can take immediate action to optimize performance or scale resources as necessary.

Scalability is an important factor to consider during deployment. While low-code/no-code platforms simplify the development process, ensuring that the application can handle increased traffic, data, or users requires proper scaling configurations. For applications deployed in the cloud, many platforms offer automatic scaling, meaning that the application can adjust its resources (such as processing power or storage) based on real-time demand. However, even with these features, businesses should ensure that their applications are designed to scale effectively. This involves optimizing the application's workflows, database queries, and integrations to prevent performance issues as the application grows.

Security is another crucial aspect of deploying low-code/no-code applications. These platforms often include built-in security features such as role-based access control, data encryption, and authentication mechanisms, which help secure the application and protect sensitive data. During deployment, businesses must configure these security settings to ensure that only authorized users can access specific features or data within the application. Additionally, regular security audits and updates are necessary to identify and address any vulnerabilities that may arise. Since low-code/no-code platforms often integrate with external systems, ensuring that these integrations are secure is also vital. For example, if the application connects to a customer database, businesses must ensure that the data is securely transmitted and stored according to industry standards and regulations.

As businesses continue to use low-code/no-code platforms for application deployment, it is important to establish a process for maintaining and updating deployed applications. One of the advantages of these platforms is that updates can be deployed quickly and with minimal disruption. Whether the business needs to fix bugs, add new features, or make performance improvements, low-code/no-code platforms provide tools that allow businesses to push updates without significant downtime. These updates can often be rolled out incrementally, with the ability to test new features in staging environments before they go live. This flexibility allows businesses to maintain an agile approach to application development and respond quickly to changing needs or market conditions.

Documentation is an often-overlooked aspect of the deployment process. Proper documentation ensures that all stakeholders— whether developers, business users, or IT staff—understand the structure, functionality, and configuration of the deployed application. Most low-code/no-code platforms generate some level of documentation automatically, such as details about workflows, integrations, and configurations. However, businesses should also maintain internal documentation for any customizations, special configurations, or security settings. This documentation helps ensure that the application can be properly maintained, updated, and scaled in the future and provides a useful reference in case issues arise.

Deploying low-code and no-code applications provides businesses with the ability to quickly bring innovative solutions to life, but it also requires thoughtful planning and execution. While the platform simplifies the deployment process, businesses must still ensure that proper testing, configuration, and monitoring are in place to guarantee the application's success. By focusing on security, scalability, and performance, businesses can ensure that their low-code/no-code applications are reliable and effective at meeting their goals. Additionally, maintaining ongoing monitoring and support after deployment is essential for ensuring that the application continues to meet business needs and operates efficiently as the organization grows.

Integrating AI and Machine Learning into Low-Code/No-Code Applications

The integration of artificial intelligence (AI) and machine learning (ML) into low-code and no-code applications has transformed the way businesses create, deploy, and maintain applications. These technologies are no longer limited to specialized developers or data scientists. Low-code and no-code platforms have made it easier for non-technical users to incorporate AI and ML models into their applications, enabling organizations to unlock the full potential of their data and enhance their processes without requiring deep technical expertise. By embedding AI and ML functionalities into applications, businesses can automate decision-making, improve user experiences, and drive efficiencies across various operations.

Low-code and no-code platforms simplify the process of integrating AI and ML by providing pre-built connectors, components, and APIs that make it possible to include advanced analytics and predictive models in applications without writing complex code. These platforms often offer direct integration with popular AI and ML tools, such as Google Cloud AI, Microsoft Azure Cognitive Services, and IBM Watson, allowing users to quickly add capabilities like image recognition, natural language processing (NLP), and predictive analytics to their applications. The power of AI and ML is now accessible to a broader audience, making it easier for businesses to use data to drive smarter decisions and optimize operations.

One of the key benefits of integrating AI and ML into low-code/no-code applications is automation. Machine learning models, especially those built for predictive analytics or recommendation engines, can automate many tasks that would otherwise require human intervention. For instance, an e-commerce platform can use AI-driven recommendations to suggest products to customers based on their browsing history and preferences. Similarly, businesses can use machine learning models to analyze customer interactions and predict which leads are most likely to convert into sales. These applications not only reduce the need for manual intervention but also help businesses operate more efficiently by making decisions faster and with greater accuracy.

Another area where AI and ML can add significant value to low-code/no-code applications is data analysis. In many industries, businesses collect vast amounts of data that are often difficult to process and analyze manually. By integrating machine learning algorithms, businesses can automatically analyze this data to uncover insights, trends, and patterns that would otherwise remain hidden. For example, AI can be used to detect anomalies in financial transactions, helping organizations identify fraudulent activities in real-time. Similarly, machine learning models can be employed to segment customers based on purchasing behavior, enabling businesses to personalize marketing strategies more effectively. These AI and ML capabilities allow businesses to make data-driven decisions that improve customer experiences and operational efficiencies.

Natural language processing (NLP) is another powerful application of AI and ML in low-code and no-code platforms. NLP allows machines to understand, interpret, and generate human language, making it an essential tool for improving user interactions with applications. With NLP capabilities, businesses can integrate chatbots or virtual assistants into their applications to provide customers with real-time support or assistance. These AI-powered tools can handle a wide range of queries, from answering frequently asked questions to processing customer service requests, freeing up human agents to focus on more complex tasks. Additionally, NLP can be used for sentiment analysis, allowing businesses to gauge customer emotions from text data, such as social media posts or reviews. By incorporating NLP into their applications, businesses can enhance user engagement and deliver more personalized experiences.

Low-code and no-code platforms also provide tools to help businesses integrate computer vision capabilities, which are powered by AI and ML. Computer vision allows machines to interpret and analyze visual data, such as images or video streams. This technology can be integrated into low-code applications to automate tasks like image classification, object detection, and facial recognition. For example, in the retail sector, computer vision can be used to track inventory levels by analyzing images of shelves, automatically notifying staff when items need restocking. In healthcare, medical imaging can be processed using AI models to assist doctors in diagnosing conditions such as tumors or abnormalities in scans. By embedding computer vision capabilities into applications, businesses can enhance their ability to process visual data and improve efficiency in areas such as quality control, security, and healthcare.

AI and ML also enable low-code/no-code applications to evolve and improve over time. Machine learning models are typically trained on historical data, allowing them to learn and make predictions based on patterns in the data. As more data becomes available, these models can be retrained to improve their accuracy and adapt to changing conditions. Low-code and no-code platforms often provide built-in tools for managing this retraining process, enabling businesses to continuously enhance the performance of their applications. For example, a business using a machine learning model to predict customer churn can retrain the model periodically to ensure that it remains accurate as new customer data is collected. This ongoing improvement ensures that the AI-powered application remains effective as the business grows and changes.

Despite the significant benefits that AI and ML bring to low-code/no-code applications, organizations must be mindful of the challenges and limitations associated with their integration. One of the primary challenges is ensuring that the data used to train AI models is accurate, complete, and free from bias. Machine learning models are only as good as the data they are trained on, and poor-quality data can lead to inaccurate predictions and biased outcomes. Therefore, it is essential for businesses to ensure that their data is properly cleaned, validated, and processed before it is used in AI and ML models. Low-code/no-code platforms often provide tools for managing data quality, such as data connectors and data cleansing features, but businesses must still be vigilant about the integrity of the data they use.

Another challenge is ensuring that AI and ML models are interpretable and explainable. In some industries, particularly those that deal with sensitive data like finance or healthcare, regulations require businesses to be able to explain how their AI models make decisions. Black-box models, which provide predictions without offering insights into the reasoning behind them, can be difficult to interpret and may not meet regulatory requirements. Low-code and no-code platforms that integrate AI and ML models often provide some level of transparency, but businesses may still need to work closely with data scientists or AI specialists to ensure that the models they use are explainable and compliant with industry regulations.

Security is also a critical consideration when integrating AI and ML into low-code/no-code applications. AI models can be vulnerable to adversarial attacks, where malicious actors manipulate the input data to trick the model into making incorrect predictions. Businesses must implement security measures to protect their AI models and ensure that they are not susceptible to such attacks. This includes securing the data used for training the models, implementing encryption for data in transit and at rest, and ensuring that only authorized users can access the models and modify them. Low-code and no-code platforms often include built-in security features, but businesses must remain vigilant about securing their AI-powered applications.

Integrating AI and machine learning into low-code and no-code applications opens up a world of possibilities for businesses, enabling them to automate decision-making, improve user experiences, and unlock valuable insights from their data. By leveraging these technologies, businesses can enhance their operations, reduce costs, and deliver personalized solutions to customers. While challenges exist, the ability to integrate AI and ML into applications without requiring extensive technical expertise empowers businesses to innovate quickly and stay ahead of the competition. As AI and ML continue to evolve, low-code and no-code platforms will play an increasingly important role in helping businesses adopt and integrate these technologies into their workflows.

Best Practices for Building Scalable Low-Code/No-Code Apps

Low-code and no-code platforms have revolutionized the way applications are developed, offering a simplified process that allows business users and non-technical teams to create applications without writing complex code. While these platforms offer an intuitive approach to development, it is essential to understand the best practices for building scalable applications to ensure they can handle increased user demand, growing data, and evolving business needs. Scalability is critical for ensuring that applications remain performant, reliable, and secure as they grow. By adhering to best practices during the development process, businesses can create low-code and no-code applications that can scale efficiently without sacrificing quality or performance.

One of the first steps in building scalable low-code and no-code applications is to define clear objectives and understand the expected growth of the application. Knowing the goals of the application and how it will be used can help guide decisions regarding architecture, design, and infrastructure. When designing an application, it is important to anticipate how the app will scale over time. For example, if the application is expected to handle a large volume of users or data, the design should take into account how it will handle increased traffic, concurrent users, and large datasets. A scalable application must be able to adapt as the business expands, so planning ahead for future needs is essential.

One of the core considerations when designing scalable applications is the platform's ability to integrate seamlessly with external systems. Most low-code and no-code applications are not stand-alone solutions but are designed to work with other systems, such as CRM platforms, databases, and third-party services. Ensuring that the application can integrate easily with these systems is a key factor in scalability. As business requirements evolve, the need for additional integrations may arise, and it is essential that the application can adapt and integrate with new tools without requiring significant redesign. Many low-code and no-code platforms come with pre-built connectors or API integrations, which can help businesses create scalable solutions. However, it is important to consider how these integrations will function as the volume of data and interactions increases. The use of lightweight, efficient APIs and ensuring proper error handling for integrations is crucial to avoid performance bottlenecks.

Another important consideration is data management. Scalable low-code and no-code applications must be able to handle increasing amounts of data over time. This involves implementing strategies for data storage, retrieval, and processing that ensure efficient performance even as the amount of data grows. Low-code and no-code platforms often provide options for connecting to databases, but it is essential to choose the right database architecture and structure for the needs of the application. When designing the application's data model, consider how it will scale. For instance, using relational databases may be appropriate for certain types of applications, while other use cases may benefit from NoSQL databases that are better suited for handling large volumes of unstructured data. Proper indexing, data normalization, and data integrity checks will help ensure that the application can manage and retrieve large datasets efficiently without compromising performance.

User interface (UI) design plays a significant role in the scalability of an application. While low-code and no-code platforms often provide pre-designed components and templates, it is important to ensure that the UI is designed for performance. As the application scales, the complexity of the UI can impact its performance, especially when handling a large number of users or data-heavy components such as tables, charts, or images. For scalable applications, it is important to keep the UI responsive and optimized. This can be achieved by using lightweight components, lazy loading (loading content only when needed), and minimizing the use of complex or resource-intensive visual elements. It is also important to consider the application's performance across different devices and screen sizes, ensuring that the design is responsive and can adapt to various environments without causing delays or disruptions for the end-user.

Security is another critical aspect of scalability. As applications scale, the need to ensure that sensitive data and user information are protected becomes even more important. Low-code and no-code applications often include built-in security features such as role-based access control (RBAC), encryption, and authentication mechanisms. However, it is essential to ensure that these security features are properly configured and continuously updated to protect against emerging threats. For applications that handle sensitive data, compliance with regulations such as GDPR, HIPAA, or PCI-DSS should be a priority. As the application scales, it is important to monitor security vulnerabilities and implement measures to ensure that the application remains secure even as it handles more users, data, and integrations. Implementing robust logging and audit trails for monitoring user activity and access to sensitive data is also crucial for maintaining security at scale.

Another practice for ensuring scalability is to design the application with modularity in mind. Low-code and no-code platforms enable users to build applications quickly, but as the application evolves, it may require modifications or the addition of new features. By designing the application in a modular way, businesses can easily add new functionality or update existing features without disrupting the entire system. This could involve using reusable components, modular workflows, and clear separation of concerns within the application's architecture. For example, a business may want to integrate new payment processing functionality or extend the app with additional reporting features in the future. By building the application in a modular fashion, the development team can add these features without requiring significant rework or downtime.

Performance testing is an essential part of ensuring scalability. Before deployment, the application should undergo rigorous testing to evaluate how it performs under different levels of stress and load. This testing helps identify potential bottlenecks or areas where the application might fail as the user base grows. Many low-code and no-code platforms provide built-in tools for performance testing, allowing users to simulate different levels of traffic, data input, and user interactions. Testing should cover various scenarios, such as peak usage times, large data uploads, and multiple concurrent users, to ensure that the application can handle these conditions without compromising user experience or performance. This proactive approach to performance testing can help businesses identify and address issues before they impact end-users.

Ongoing monitoring and optimization are also vital for maintaining scalability as the application grows. After deployment, businesses should continuously monitor the application's performance, user interactions, and data usage to ensure that it continues to meet performance expectations. Many low-code and no-code platforms provide monitoring dashboards that give insights into key metrics such as load times, user activity, and server resources. By regularly reviewing these metrics, businesses can quickly identify areas for improvement and make adjustments as necessary. Scaling an application is an ongoing process, and the ability to respond to changes in user behavior, data volume, and application performance will help businesses maintain a reliable and high-performing solution over time.

The ability to scale low-code and no-code applications requires a combination of strategic planning, sound design practices, and continuous monitoring. By understanding the potential challenges and proactively implementing solutions, businesses can ensure that their applications are not only efficient and effective at launch but can continue to grow and adapt to changing business needs. The flexibility and accessibility provided by low-code and no-code platforms enable businesses to quickly build scalable solutions that deliver value now and in the future. With the right approach, businesses can harness the full power of these platforms and create applications that can scale seamlessly as their needs evolve.

Low-Code/No-Code Development for Mobile Applications

The growing demand for mobile applications has driven the evolution of development tools and platforms, with low-code and no-code platforms emerging as powerful solutions for businesses seeking to quickly and efficiently create mobile applications. These platforms have democratized the app development process, allowing users with limited or no coding experience to design, build, and deploy mobile applications. Traditionally, building mobile apps required specialized knowledge of programming languages and mobile development frameworks. Low-code and no-code platforms have simplified this process by offering visual interfaces, pre-built components, and drag-and-drop functionality, allowing developers and business users alike to create mobile applications tailored to their specific needs.

Low-code and no-code development for mobile applications streamlines the entire process, from design to deployment. One of the key benefits is the speed at which applications can be developed. In traditional app development, the process of writing code, testing, debugging, and deploying can take weeks or even months, especially for complex applications. With low-code and no-code platforms, users can leverage pre-built templates and modules to quickly create mobile applications, significantly reducing the development timeline. These platforms often come with customizable templates that are optimized for mobile devices, allowing users to focus on the layout and functionality rather than the technical details of mobile app development.

These platforms also offer the advantage of being user-friendly, which allows business users and non-technical teams to contribute to the mobile app development process. A marketing manager, for example, might be able to create a custom mobile app that integrates with their company's CRM system to provide mobile access to customer data, all without needing to write a single line of code. This ease of use empowers teams outside of the IT department to take ownership of app development, accelerating time-to-market and ensuring that the application is tailored to the needs of the business. With the drag-and-drop functionality offered by these platforms, users can add features like forms, buttons, navigation bars, and image galleries with minimal effort, resulting in a functional mobile app in a fraction of the time it would take using traditional development methods.

One of the most important aspects of developing mobile applications is ensuring they are responsive and optimized for a variety of screen sizes, operating systems, and devices. Low-code and no-code platforms cater to this need by offering responsive design features that automatically adjust the app's layout based on the screen size and resolution of the device. This eliminates the need for developers to manually create separate versions of the app for iOS, Android, or tablet devices. As mobile usage continues to increase across different types of devices, the ability to create apps that seamlessly work across various platforms is essential. These platforms help businesses create mobile apps that maintain a consistent user experience across all devices, ensuring that the app performs optimally on smartphones, tablets, and even desktop browsers when necessary.

In addition to ease of design, low-code and no-code platforms allow for rapid iteration and testing, which is essential for developing successful mobile applications. Given the fast-paced nature of the mobile app market, businesses need to continuously test and refine their apps based on user feedback and emerging trends. Low-code and no-code platforms allow users to make quick adjustments to the app, such as adding new features, adjusting the user interface, or fixing bugs, all without significant delays. These platforms often include built-in testing tools that allow businesses to simulate mobile environments and test how the app will behave on different devices and operating systems. This iterative approach to development ensures that businesses can deliver a mobile app that meets the needs of their users while keeping pace with changing expectations.

Another advantage of low-code and no-code platforms for mobile application development is the ability to easily integrate with external systems and services. Many mobile apps require integrations with third-party services, such as payment gateways, customer relationship management (CRM) systems, social media platforms, or cloud storage solutions. Traditionally, building these integrations would require significant development effort and expertise. However, low-code and no-code platforms come with pre-built connectors and integration tools that simplify the process. Users can integrate services like PayPal for payments, Google Drive for cloud storage, or Salesforce for customer data without writing custom code. This ability to quickly integrate with external systems enhances the functionality of mobile applications and makes it easier for businesses to create solutions that connect with their existing workflows and infrastructure.

Security is a critical concern in mobile app development, particularly as mobile devices are often used to access sensitive information, such as personal data, payment details, and private company data. Low-code and no-code platforms understand the importance of security and often come with built-in security features to help safeguard the data and integrity of mobile apps. These platforms typically include options for user authentication, data encryption, and secure access controls, ensuring that only authorized users can access certain features or data. Many platforms also comply with industry standards and regulations, such as GDPR or HIPAA, to help businesses meet legal requirements for data protection and privacy. This built-in security reduces the complexity of implementing secure mobile apps and ensures that businesses can focus on delivering value to their users without compromising security.

Despite their many advantages, low-code and no-code platforms for mobile application development do have some limitations. While these platforms are excellent for building basic and moderately complex apps, they may not be suitable for applications that require highly custom features or complex back-end logic. For example, if a business requires real-time data processing or complex algorithms, low-code or no-code tools may fall short in providing the necessary capabilities. In such cases, developers may still need to write custom code or work with traditional development frameworks to build the required functionality. However, for most use cases, low-code and no-code platforms offer sufficient flexibility and customization options to build robust, feature-rich mobile applications without the need for extensive coding knowledge.

Low-code and no-code platforms also provide opportunities for businesses to scale their mobile applications over time. As user demand increases or new features are needed, these platforms allow businesses to adapt and enhance their applications with minimal effort. With the ability to modify workflows, integrate new tools, and update user interfaces, businesses can continue to evolve their mobile apps as their needs change. This scalability is particularly valuable in industries that experience rapid changes or need to frequently update their applications to stay competitive.

Furthermore, many low-code and no-code platforms offer cloud-based deployment options, which makes it easier for businesses to distribute their mobile apps to a global audience. Once the app is built, it can be deployed to the App Store or Google Play Store with minimal hassle. These platforms often handle the backend infrastructure, ensuring that the app is scalable, reliable, and able to handle increasing traffic without significant technical intervention. This cloud-based approach simplifies the deployment process and ensures that businesses can focus on delivering a great user experience rather than managing infrastructure.

In summary, low-code and no-code platforms have made mobile application development more accessible than ever before, allowing businesses to rapidly create and deploy mobile apps without the need for extensive programming expertise. By offering visual design tools, pre-built components, and seamless integrations, these platforms enable users to quickly build mobile applications that meet their specific business needs. While these platforms are best suited for certain types of apps, they offer a powerful solution for many organizations looking to improve their mobile presence and deliver valuable features to their users with speed and efficiency. As these platforms continue to evolve, they will likely play an even greater role in shaping the future of mobile app development.

Creating Business Applications with Low-Code/No-Code Platforms

Low-code and no-code platforms have drastically reshaped the landscape of application development, offering businesses an opportunity to build customized solutions with minimal or no programming knowledge. This democratization of app development has proven to be transformative, especially for businesses looking to quickly adapt to changing market demands without relying on traditional, resource-heavy development cycles. These platforms offer intuitive interfaces, pre-built templates, and automation tools that empower both business users and IT teams to develop applications that streamline processes, enhance customer experiences, and improve operational efficiencies.

Creating business applications with low-code and no-code platforms starts with the realization that these tools enable a wide range of users to take an active role in the development process. Business users, analysts, and department heads who understand the intricacies of business operations can directly contribute to the creation of applications without needing to rely on development teams. This direct involvement allows applications to be better aligned with the needs of the business, as users can tailor solutions to specific requirements without needing to pass through multiple layers of communication. For example, an HR manager could build an employee onboarding system, or a sales manager could create a custom CRM tool, each without having to consult developers for every change.

The simplicity and accessibility of low-code and no-code platforms do not limit the complexity or functionality of the applications created with them. These platforms provide a variety of tools for building everything from simple forms and data collection systems to more complex business process automation systems, customer relationship management solutions, and enterprise resource planning tools. The platform typically offers drag-and-drop features, allowing users to visually design workflows, databases, user interfaces, and logic structures without needing to write code. While the user interface and workflow configuration is intuitive, these platforms are built to handle a wide range of use cases, supporting integrations with external systems, automation of repetitive tasks, and real-time data processing. This scalability allows businesses to create solutions that not only meet current needs but are also flexible enough to grow as the business evolves.

A key aspect of business application creation with low-code and no-code platforms is the ability to automate processes. Business applications often require workflows that facilitate the automation of repetitive tasks, such as data entry, approval processes, or communications with clients. Low-code and no-code platforms provide powerful workflow automation tools that allow businesses to design processes that trigger actions based on specific conditions or events. For instance, in an inventory management system, a business application could automatically notify the appropriate team member when stock levels fall below a certain threshold, or trigger an email to customers when their order is shipped. By automating these workflows, businesses can reduce human error, increase operational efficiency, and ensure that processes are completed in a timely manner.

Another important feature of low-code and no-code platforms for business applications is the ability to integrate with existing systems and databases. Many organizations use a range of software solutions, such as CRMs, ERPs, accounting systems, and customer support tools, to manage different aspects of their business. In a traditional development environment, integrating these systems could be a complex and time-consuming task, often requiring custom development for each integration. However, low-code and no-code platforms offer pre-built connectors and API integration tools that simplify this process, enabling applications to connect seamlessly with external systems. For example, a business could integrate a custom application with their existing CRM to pull customer data into the new tool, or link an accounting software system to automate financial reporting. These integrations enhance the functionality of business applications, allowing them to interact with data from multiple sources in real-time and reducing the need for manual data entry or duplication of work.

Security and compliance are critical considerations when building business applications, especially those that handle sensitive data or are subject to industry regulations. Low-code and no-code platforms often come with built-in security features, such as role-based access control, user authentication, and data encryption. These features ensure that only authorized users can access specific parts of the application, protecting both the data and the business. Additionally, many platforms are designed with compliance in mind, supporting industry standards such as GDPR, HIPAA, and PCI-DSS. This compliance support can significantly reduce the complexity of developing business applications that meet regulatory requirements, allowing businesses to focus on delivering functionality without worrying about security vulnerabilities or legal concerns.

Customization is another key benefit of using low-code and no-code platforms to build business applications. While these platforms provide pre-built templates and components that can be used as starting points, they also offer flexibility for customization. Users can modify templates to meet specific business needs, create custom forms, design unique workflows, and integrate additional functionality. This level of customization ensures that the application closely aligns with the company's processes, branding, and goals. Businesses can also extend the functionality of their applications by adding custom code when needed. This hybrid approach allows non-technical users to build applications quickly while still giving more technical teams the ability to implement advanced features or fine-tune the application for specific requirements.

Performance is a crucial aspect when building business applications that can handle increasing user demands, large datasets, and high transaction volumes. Many low-code and no-code platforms are cloud-based, which allows for easy scalability. As the business grows and the number of users increases, cloud infrastructure can dynamically allocate additional resources to ensure that the application performs optimally. These platforms typically offer built-in tools to monitor application performance in real time, allowing businesses to identify potential bottlenecks or areas of concern. Whether the application is used by a handful of internal users or needs to support a large customer base, the scalability of the platform ensures that it can handle growth efficiently without requiring a complete redesign or infrastructure overhaul.

Testing and iteration are essential components of the application development process. Low-code and no-code platforms often provide built-in testing environments where users can simulate real-world usage scenarios to identify issues before deployment. This includes functional testing to ensure the application works as intended, as well as performance testing to check how the app behaves under heavy usage. These testing features allow businesses to continuously refine and improve their applications based on feedback, ensuring that the final product meets user expectations and business requirements.

After the application is deployed, businesses must maintain and update it regularly to ensure it continues to meet the evolving needs of the business. Low-code and no-code platforms make it easy to update applications, whether it's adding new features, improving performance, or making changes to workflows. These platforms often support version control and allow users to roll back changes if needed, providing flexibility and reducing the risk of downtime or errors. Additionally, businesses can continue to gather feedback from users, monitor the application's performance, and make adjustments as necessary to ensure the application remains relevant and functional over time.

Low-code and no-code platforms have revolutionized the way businesses approach application development. By offering a user-friendly, accessible way to build business applications, these platforms empower non-technical users to create custom solutions that streamline processes, automate workflows, and improve operational efficiency. The ability to integrate with existing systems, automate tasks, ensure security and compliance, and customize applications makes low-code and no-code platforms an invaluable tool for businesses looking to develop innovative solutions quickly and cost-effectively. With the right approach, businesses can harness the full potential of these platforms to drive success and growth in today's fast-paced, technology-driven world.

Integrating APIs and Web Services in Low-Code/No-Code Solutions

In the modern landscape of application development, integration with external systems is often essential for building effective and functional solutions. Low-code and no-code platforms have simplified the process of creating applications by enabling users to build solutions quickly without deep coding expertise. However, to meet the dynamic needs of businesses, it is frequently necessary to integrate these solutions with external systems and services, such as databases, third-party applications, or web services. This is where the integration of APIs (Application Programming Interfaces) and web services plays a crucial role. By leveraging these technologies, businesses can extend the capabilities of their low-code and no-code applications, making them more robust, data-driven, and interconnected with other business systems.

APIs and web services are fundamental building blocks that enable applications to communicate with other systems over a network. While APIs typically refer to a set of protocols and tools that allow different software applications to interact, web services are a broader concept that includes any type of software service that enables communication over the internet. They can use protocols like HTTP and REST, which are common in web development, or other communication protocols such as SOAP (Simple Object Access Protocol). APIs and web services allow applications to exchange data, perform actions, and access remote resources, thereby enabling integration with third-party services like payment gateways, customer relationship management (CRM) systems, or cloud storage.

Low-code and no-code platforms simplify the integration of these external services by providing pre-built connectors and integration tools that make it possible to connect applications to APIs and web services without writing complex code. Many of these platforms offer visual interfaces, where users can define API calls, map data between external systems and the application, and configure how data should flow between services. For example, a user might use a pre-built connector in a low-code platform to connect a customer data management system like Salesforce to their application, allowing the app to pull customer data automatically without requiring manual entry. This seamless integration enhances the application's functionality, allowing businesses to streamline operations, reduce errors, and improve data consistency.

The integration of APIs and web services into low-code and no-code applications is particularly important for businesses that rely on multiple software systems. In a typical business environment, companies may use different tools for various functions, such as inventory management, accounting, and customer support. These systems often need to exchange data in real time, and APIs and web services make this possible. By integrating external systems into a low-code or no-code application, businesses can automate data flows and eliminate the need for manual data entry, which can save time, reduce errors, and increase overall efficiency. For example, if a business uses an online payment gateway like Stripe or PayPal, integrating the payment system via an API allows the low-code application to automatically process transactions and update inventory levels without requiring any manual intervention.

One of the most powerful benefits of using APIs and web services in low-code and no-code solutions is the ability to scale and enhance the application over time. As businesses grow and their needs evolve, they often require new features or need to integrate with additional systems. Low-code and no-code platforms make it easy to add new integrations as business requirements change, without the need to completely overhaul the application. For instance, if a business initially integrates an email marketing platform like Mailchimp but later needs to incorporate an SMS marketing tool, the low-code platform can allow for seamless integration of new services. This ability to scale and adapt by integrating new APIs and web services ensures that low-code and no-code applications can evolve alongside the business.

The process of integrating APIs and web services into low-code/no-code applications often involves defining how data is transferred and how external systems interact with the application. One key element of this integration is mapping data fields between the external service and the low-code application. For example, when integrating a CRM system like HubSpot into a custom app, the user may need to map fields such as customer name, email address, and purchase history between the two systems. This mapping ensures that the data is correctly interpreted and that the systems can work together in a cohesive manner. Low-code platforms typically provide a user-friendly interface to perform this data mapping, reducing the complexity of integration tasks and making it accessible to business users who may not have technical expertise.

While integrating APIs and web services into low-code and no-code applications is typically a simplified process, businesses must still consider certain best practices to ensure smooth integration. First and foremost, proper authentication and security mechanisms should be implemented. Many external services require secure access through mechanisms such as API keys, OAuth tokens, or other forms of authentication. It is important to follow best practices for securing these credentials, such as storing them in encrypted variables or using secure authentication protocols to prevent unauthorized access to sensitive data. Many low-code and no-code platforms include built-in security features to help manage these credentials and provide encryption, which makes it easier for businesses to comply with industry standards and protect their data.

Error handling is another critical aspect when integrating APIs and web services into applications. APIs and web services can occasionally fail, whether due to network issues, incorrect data formats, or system downtime. It is important for businesses to implement error handling strategies that allow the application to gracefully handle failures and provide meaningful error messages to users. Low-code platforms often allow users to configure error handling workflows, such as retrying failed API calls or notifying users when an integration fails. These measures ensure that the application remains stable, even when issues arise with external services, and help users quickly resolve any problems that may occur.

Another consideration in API and web service integration is rate limiting and performance optimization. Many APIs and web services impose limits on the number of requests that can be made within a specific time frame, known as rate limits. Businesses must be mindful of these limitations when designing their applications to avoid exceeding the allowed number of requests, which could lead to temporary service disruptions or additional costs. Additionally, integrating APIs and web services can sometimes impact the performance of the application, particularly when dealing with large datasets or complex integrations. To optimize performance, businesses should implement strategies such as caching frequently accessed data or batching API requests to minimize the number of calls to external services.

Monitoring and maintaining integrations over time is another key aspect of successful API and web service integration. APIs and web services may evolve, with updates or changes to endpoints, data formats, or authentication methods. Regular monitoring ensures that the application continues to function correctly as external systems change. Many low-code and no-code platforms offer tools for tracking API usage and performance, which can help businesses identify potential issues early. Additionally, keeping up with updates to the APIs and web services integrated into the application is essential to ensure compatibility and continued functionality.

The integration of APIs and web services into low-code and no-code solutions provides businesses with a powerful way to create more dynamic, data-driven applications. These integrations enable applications to interact with external systems, automate workflows, and enhance functionality without requiring extensive custom development. By using pre-built connectors, mapping data, and ensuring proper security and error handling, businesses can seamlessly integrate third-party services and build robust solutions. As businesses continue to rely on a diverse ecosystem of tools and services, the ability to integrate APIs and web services into low-code and no-code applications will remain a key factor in creating scalable and effective solutions.

How Low-Code/No-Code Platforms Promote Rapid Prototyping

In today's fast-paced business environment, the ability to quickly develop and iterate on prototypes has become essential for companies aiming to innovate and stay ahead of the competition. Low-code and no-code platforms have emerged as game-changers in this regard, enabling organizations to create functional prototypes in a fraction of the time it would take using traditional development methods. These platforms allow users with little to no programming experience to quickly design, test, and refine ideas, making the process of prototyping more accessible and efficient than ever before. By simplifying the development process and reducing the need for complex coding, low-code and no-code platforms promote rapid prototyping, allowing businesses to bring their ideas to life quickly and adjust them based on feedback.

The key advantage of low-code and no-code platforms is that they enable non-technical users, such as business analysts, product managers, and marketing teams, to actively participate in the prototyping process. In traditional development environments, the prototyping phase often requires collaboration between business users and developers, which can lead to delays in communication, misunderstandings, and longer development cycles. However, with low-code and no-code platforms, these business stakeholders can directly create and modify prototypes without relying on developers for every change. This reduces the time spent on back-and-forth communication, allowing teams to rapidly iterate and adjust the prototype according to evolving requirements. The visual, drag-and-drop interfaces of these platforms allow users to quickly design user interfaces, workflows, and logic without needing extensive technical knowledge, resulting in faster turnaround times for prototypes.

Rapid prototyping is crucial for businesses looking to validate ideas, gather feedback, and test concepts before committing significant resources to full-scale development. Low-code and no-code platforms facilitate this by allowing teams to build functional prototypes that simulate the core features and user experiences of the final product. These prototypes can be deployed and tested in real-world scenarios, giving stakeholders the ability to evaluate the viability of a concept early in the development process. For example, a company might want to test a new customer service app that includes specific workflows and user interactions. Instead of spending months developing the app from scratch, the team can use a low-code platform to build a prototype in a matter of days, test it with users, and refine it based on their feedback. This iterative approach not only speeds up the process but also ensures that the final product is more closely aligned with user needs and expectations.

The ability to quickly iterate on prototypes is a fundamental characteristic of the low-code and no-code development process. These platforms allow users to make real-time changes to prototypes, such as adjusting workflows, modifying user interfaces, or adding new features, without requiring a complete redevelopment of the app. Traditional development methods often involve long cycles of coding, testing, and debugging, which can slow down the process of making changes. With low-code and no-code platforms, users can quickly modify their prototypes in response to new insights or feedback, testing out different design options or functionalities with minimal delay. This rapid iteration helps businesses experiment with different approaches, refine their ideas, and discover the most effective solutions in a fraction of the time.

Another significant benefit of low-code and no-code platforms for rapid prototyping is the ability to integrate with external data sources and services. Prototypes are most useful when they simulate real-world conditions, and integrating external data allows teams to test their ideas in a more realistic environment. These platforms often come with pre-built connectors and API integration tools that enable users to pull in data from other systems, such as customer databases, payment gateways, or analytics platforms. This integration capability allows prototypes to not only simulate core functionality but also interact with actual data, making the testing process more accurate and meaningful. For example, a business can integrate a payment gateway into a prototype of an e-commerce app, allowing it to test the payment process with real transactions, rather than relying on mock data.

Low-code and no-code platforms also promote collaboration during the prototyping process by making it easier for different teams to work together. In traditional development environments, creating a prototype typically requires collaboration between developers, designers, and business stakeholders, which can be challenging due to differences in technical expertise and communication barriers. With low-code and no-code tools, however, teams from different departments can collaborate more easily, as the platforms allow non-technical users to contribute directly to the development process. This not only accelerates the prototyping phase but also ensures that the prototype more accurately reflects the business requirements, user preferences, and design standards. Product managers, designers, and other stakeholders can all contribute to the creation and refinement of the prototype, ensuring that it aligns with the overall vision for the product.

The visual nature of low-code and no-code platforms is another key factor in promoting rapid prototyping. These platforms typically offer intuitive, drag-and-drop interfaces that allow users to quickly assemble the elements of their prototype. By visually designing the user interface, defining workflows, and configuring data models, users can easily create prototypes that are both functional and visually appealing. This visual approach not only speeds up the process of building prototypes but also makes it easier for non-technical users to understand and engage with the design. It allows business users to see the prototype in action, giving them a clearer understanding of how the final product will function and enabling them to provide more informed feedback.

Low-code and no-code platforms also support the rapid deployment of prototypes. Once a prototype is built, it can often be deployed to a testing environment or even to end-users with just a few clicks. This quick deployment allows businesses to validate their prototypes in real-world scenarios, gather user feedback, and make adjustments as necessary. The ability to deploy and test prototypes quickly is a key advantage, as it allows businesses to test different concepts and features without the need for lengthy development cycles. This rapid deployment process accelerates the feedback loop, enabling teams to make informed decisions faster and reducing the time spent on trial and error.

Additionally, the cost-effectiveness of using low-code and no-code platforms for prototyping is another reason why businesses are increasingly adopting these tools. Traditional prototyping often requires a significant investment in development resources, both in terms of time and money. Low-code and no-code platforms, on the other hand, lower the cost of prototyping by reducing the need for skilled developers and accelerating the development process. This makes it more affordable for businesses of all sizes to create and test prototypes, even with limited resources. The ability to quickly test and validate ideas before committing to full-scale development ensures that businesses are investing their resources wisely, avoiding costly mistakes, and focusing on ideas that have the highest potential for success.

The ability to rapidly prototype is essential in today's fast-moving business environment. Low-code and no-code platforms enable businesses to bring ideas to life quickly, iterate based on feedback, and create products that meet the needs of users. By empowering business users to take an active role in the development process, these platforms foster collaboration, improve alignment with business goals, and reduce time-to-market. Through their ease of use, flexibility, and integration capabilities, low-code and no-code platforms are revolutionizing the way businesses approach prototyping, making it easier to test, refine, and deploy ideas that can drive innovation and growth.

Real-World Examples of Low-Code/No-Code Application Development

Low-code and no-code platforms have fundamentally changed the way businesses approach application development by allowing individuals with little or no coding experience to create functional and efficient applications. These platforms have made application development more accessible, enabling businesses to quickly respond to market demands, automate workflows, and build solutions without waiting for traditional development cycles. Across various industries, low-code and no-code tools have been leveraged to solve real-world business problems, streamline operations, and innovate faster than ever before.

One notable example of low-code application development is in the healthcare sector, where these platforms are used to automate administrative tasks, improve patient management, and enhance overall efficiency. Healthcare providers face significant challenges in managing patient data, scheduling appointments, and coordinating care across multiple departments. Traditionally, these tasks required complex software solutions and significant IT resources. However, by using low-code platforms, healthcare organizations have been able to develop custom applications that integrate patient information systems, appointment scheduling tools, and communication platforms. These applications help medical staff access real-time data, reduce administrative errors, and provide better care coordination. For instance, a low-code application could automatically update patient records across multiple systems, reducing the risk of duplicate data entry and improving accuracy. In this way, healthcare providers have been able to improve operational efficiency, enhance patient experiences, and comply with regulations without the long development cycles typically associated with traditional software solutions.

In the finance and banking sector, low-code and no-code platforms have been used to build applications that automate tasks like loan approval processes, customer onboarding, and fraud detection. Banks and financial institutions deal with large volumes of sensitive data, requiring robust systems to ensure compliance with regulations and security standards. Low-code platforms have enabled banks to create applications that streamline these processes while reducing human error and improving compliance. For example, a bank could develop a no-code solution that automates the approval of personal loans by integrating credit scoring models, verifying customer information, and automatically generating approval notifications. Additionally, fraud detection systems can be built using low-code platforms, leveraging machine learning models that analyze transaction patterns and identify unusual activities. These applications are deployed quickly, allowing financial institutions to improve customer service, reduce processing times, and stay competitive in a rapidly evolving market.

Retail companies have also embraced low-code and no-code tools to develop applications that enhance customer engagement, streamline inventory management, and automate supply chain operations. In retail, customer experience is a key driver of success, and businesses need to quickly adapt to changing customer preferences and market trends. Using low-code platforms, retailers can create customized mobile apps, e-commerce websites, and loyalty programs that integrate seamlessly with their back-end systems. For instance, a retail company could use a low-code platform to build a mobile app that allows customers to place orders, track shipments, and access personalized discounts based on their purchasing behavior. These applications can be deployed rapidly, enabling retailers to test new features and gather customer feedback in real-time. Similarly, inventory management applications built with low-code platforms can provide real-time updates on stock levels, automate reorder processes, and alert staff when stock runs low. These tools help retailers reduce waste, optimize inventory, and improve the overall shopping experience.

In education, low-code and no-code platforms have been used to create applications that support remote learning, manage student data, and streamline administrative tasks. With the rapid shift to online education in recent years, educational institutions have needed to adapt quickly to new technologies and provide students and teachers with seamless learning experiences. Low-code platforms allow educators to develop custom learning management systems (LMS), class scheduling tools, and student assessment applications that can be easily integrated with existing school databases and tools. For example, a university could use a low-code platform to build a custom student portal where students can access course materials, submit assignments, and track their academic progress. These tools help educational institutions deliver personalized learning experiences, improve administrative efficiency, and enhance communication between students and faculty. The flexibility of low-code/no-code platforms also enables schools to adapt their applications as needs change, ensuring that they remain aligned with evolving educational standards and practices.

Nonprofit organizations have found tremendous value in low-code and no-code platforms for building applications that enhance donor management, automate fundraising campaigns, and track volunteer activities. Nonprofits often operate on limited budgets and resources, which makes the ability to develop applications without relying on expensive IT teams essential. With low-code tools, nonprofit organizations can create applications that automate donation tracking, generate fundraising reports, and allow donors to easily contribute through online portals. For example, a nonprofit could use a low-code platform to build a custom donation page that integrates with payment processors, automatically generates receipts, and tracks donation history. These platforms also enable nonprofits to create event management tools, allowing them to organize volunteer opportunities, track attendance, and send automated reminders to participants. By utilizing low-code and no-code platforms, nonprofit organizations can enhance their efficiency, increase donor engagement, and focus on their mission without needing to invest heavily in custom software development.

The manufacturing industry is another sector that benefits from the capabilities of low-code and no-code platforms. Manufacturers have complex processes involving inventory management, production scheduling, quality control, and supply chain management. Low-code applications allow manufacturers to streamline these processes by integrating data from various sources, automating workflows, and improving communication across departments. For instance, a manufacturing company could develop a no-code app that tracks the production line's progress, monitors equipment performance, and alerts staff when maintenance is needed. These applications provide real-time insights into production performance, helping businesses reduce downtime and optimize operational efficiency. Additionally, low-code platforms enable manufacturers to build custom dashboards that visualize key performance indicators (KPIs), making it easier for decision-makers to monitor performance and make data-driven decisions.

One of the most compelling advantages of low-code and no-code platforms is their ability to enable rapid prototyping and testing of new ideas. Companies across industries are using these platforms to quickly create prototypes of new applications, test them with users, and iterate based on feedback. This rapid experimentation allows businesses to validate ideas before investing significant resources into full-scale development. For example, a tech startup might use a no-code platform to build a prototype of a new mobile app, test it with a small group of users, and gather valuable insights on the user interface, features, and functionality. This iterative process of testing and refining ensures that the final product aligns with customer needs and market demand, reducing the risk of failure and accelerating time-to-market.

Across all of these industries, low-code and no-code platforms provide organizations with the ability to build custom solutions that address their unique business challenges without the need for extensive coding knowledge. By empowering business users to create applications that meet their specific needs, these platforms drive innovation, improve operational efficiency, and reduce the time and cost associated with traditional software development. Whether for automating processes, improving customer engagement, or creating custom workflows, low-code and no-code platforms have proven to be invaluable tools for businesses looking to stay competitive in today's fast-moving market. Through the use of these platforms, businesses of all sizes can harness the power of technology to transform their operations and deliver better outcomes for their customers and stakeholders.

Understanding the Role of Low-Code/No-Code in Digital Transformation

In today's rapidly changing business environment, digital transformation has become a central goal for organizations across industries. Companies are leveraging technology to improve their processes, deliver better customer experiences, and create new business models. However, the traditional methods of software development—often complex, time-consuming, and expensive—are proving to be barriers to achieving these goals. Low-code and no-code platforms have emerged as essential tools in the digital transformation process, offering businesses an accessible and efficient way to create and deploy applications without the need for deep technical expertise. These platforms have unlocked the potential for both business users and IT professionals to build powerful applications that drive innovation and enhance operational efficiency.

The role of low-code and no-code platforms in digital transformation is multifaceted. One of the primary advantages of these platforms is their ability to accelerate the development process. Traditionally, software development has required highly specialized skills, with developers writing complex code to create applications from scratch. This lengthy process often involved multiple phases of planning, coding, testing, and debugging, which could take months or even years. Low-code and no-code platforms simplify this process by providing visual interfaces that allow users to drag and drop components, configure workflows, and design user interfaces without needing to write code. This speed and ease of development enable organizations to quickly prototype new ideas, launch applications, and iterate based on feedback. By reducing development timelines, businesses can rapidly respond to market changes and stay ahead of competitors in the digital landscape.

Another key aspect of low-code and no-code platforms in digital transformation is the democratization of application development. These platforms enable business users—such as product managers, marketers, and analysts—to actively participate in the creation of applications without the need for deep technical knowledge. In traditional development environments, business users typically rely on IT teams or third-party developers to build solutions that address their needs. This often leads to long delays, miscommunication, and a lack of alignment between the business and technical teams. Low-code and no-code platforms bridge this gap by allowing non-technical users to build their own applications, customize existing solutions, and automate processes without depending on IT resources. This empowers business teams to innovate quickly and creates a more agile development environment where ideas can be tested and refined in real-time.

Moreover, low-code and no-code platforms are pivotal in addressing the growing demand for digital solutions without overwhelming IT departments. As organizations scale and their needs become more complex, the demand for new applications increases. IT departments, often already stretched thin managing existing infrastructure, may struggle to keep up with the influx of requests for new software solutions. Low-code and no-code platforms relieve some of this pressure by enabling business users to take ownership of certain development tasks, reducing the workload for IT teams. This allows IT departments to focus on more complex, high-priority tasks, while business users can quickly create solutions that address immediate needs. By decentralizing application development, businesses can scale their digital capabilities more efficiently and cost-effectively.

The scalability of low-code and no-code platforms is another reason they play a crucial role in digital transformation. These platforms are designed to scale with a business as it grows, offering the flexibility to handle increasing workloads, data, and user activity. Applications built on low-code and no-code platforms can be easily adapted, updated, and expanded as business requirements evolve. This scalability ensures that businesses can keep pace with growth and continue to deliver digital solutions that meet the changing needs of customers, employees, and stakeholders. As organizations implement more digital tools, the ability to rapidly scale applications without needing to reengineer the entire infrastructure is a significant advantage.

Low-code and no-code platforms also enhance collaboration between business and IT teams. In the past, developers and business users often worked in silos, which could lead to misunderstandings and delays in delivering solutions. With low-code and no-code platforms, business users can directly interact with the development process, providing feedback, making adjustments, and refining the application in real-time. This collaborative approach ensures that applications are aligned with business goals, user needs, and industry standards. IT teams, in turn, can oversee the platform to ensure compliance, security, and integration with existing systems. By fostering closer collaboration between business and IT, low-code and no-code platforms facilitate the creation of more effective digital solutions that drive business transformation.

The ability to integrate with existing systems is another significant factor in how low-code and no-code platforms contribute to digital transformation. In many organizations, legacy systems and applications form the backbone of business operations. While these systems may be outdated, replacing them entirely can be costly and disruptive. Low-code and no-code platforms allow businesses to create new applications that integrate seamlessly with existing systems, enabling them to modernize their technology stack incrementally. For example, a company could build a custom dashboard that pulls data from existing CRM, ERP, or financial systems, providing employees with a unified view of critical business information without needing to replace the underlying infrastructure. This ability to integrate with legacy systems helps organizations avoid costly system overhauls while still benefiting from the agility and innovation offered by digital solutions.

Security and compliance are also critical components of digital transformation, particularly for industries that handle sensitive data, such as healthcare, finance, and retail. Low-code and no-code platforms often include built-in security features such as role-based access control, encryption, and data validation, which help businesses adhere to industry regulations and protect sensitive information. Additionally, these platforms are designed to comply with various regulatory standards, such as GDPR and HIPAA, ensuring that applications meet the necessary legal requirements. By providing these security and compliance features out of the box, low-code and no-code platforms make it easier for businesses to build secure and compliant applications while focusing on innovation and growth.

The impact of low-code and no-code platforms extends beyond individual applications to the broader business strategy. As organizations embrace digital transformation, they must create a culture that values innovation, agility, and continuous improvement. Low-code and no-code platforms foster this culture by enabling rapid experimentation, iteration, and feedback. Teams can quickly prototype new ideas, test them with users, and refine them based on real-time data, all without the long delays associated with traditional development cycles. This iterative approach helps businesses remain flexible, adaptive, and responsive to market changes, which is essential for sustaining growth in a fast-paced, competitive environment.

The role of low-code and no-code platforms in digital transformation is undeniable. These platforms have provided businesses with the tools to quickly develop and deploy applications that drive efficiency, innovation, and growth. By enabling faster development cycles, fostering collaboration between business and IT teams, and offering scalability and integration with existing systems, low-code and no-code platforms are empowering organizations to embrace digital transformation more effectively than ever before. As businesses continue to rely on technology to stay competitive, the accessibility and flexibility offered by these platforms will be essential to their success in the digital age.

How to Empower Non-Technical Users with Low-Code/No-Code Tools

In today's fast-paced business world, the ability to create and manage applications without requiring deep technical knowledge has become increasingly valuable. Low-code and no-code platforms have revolutionized the way businesses operate by enabling non-technical users—such as business analysts, marketing professionals, and department heads—to build their own applications. These platforms provide intuitive, visual interfaces that allow users to design, develop, and deploy functional applications without the need for programming expertise. Empowering non-technical users with these tools not only increases operational efficiency but also accelerates innovation, as business units can create tailored solutions that address specific challenges without waiting for IT departments to prioritize their requests.

One of the primary ways to empower non-technical users with low-code and no-code tools is through user-friendly interfaces that simplify complex development processes. These platforms typically feature drag-and-drop functionality, which enables users to easily assemble applications by selecting pre-built components and placing them into a user interface. Users can quickly create forms, buttons, workflows, and data connections with minimal effort, drastically reducing the complexity traditionally associated with software development. For instance, a marketing manager can use a low-code platform to create a custom landing page that integrates with email marketing tools, all without needing to write a single line of code. The simplicity of these tools ensures that even users with little or no technical background can build applications that meet their business needs.

The visual nature of low-code and no-code platforms makes the development process more accessible and intuitive for non-technical users. These platforms typically present users with a graphical user interface (GUI) that allows them to see the structure of their application as they design it. This visual feedback enables users to easily understand how different components of the application will interact and how the user interface will appear once it is deployed. Additionally, many low-code/no-code platforms provide templates and pre-designed workflows, which further simplify the process. These templates can serve as starting points for creating applications, reducing the amount of time required to design solutions from scratch. As users modify these templates, they can see immediate changes and test how their applications will behave, further improving their understanding of how software development works.

For non-technical users to feel truly empowered, low-code and no-code platforms also need to provide ample support, including built-in guides, tutorials, and a strong user community. Many platforms offer a variety of learning resources, such as video tutorials, step-by-step guides, and community forums, which help users learn how to use the tools effectively. These resources are particularly important for users who are new to application development, as they provide clear instructions and best practices. The availability of these learning materials reduces the need for specialized training and allows non-technical users to become proficient quickly. Moreover, the presence of an active user community enables users to share ideas, ask questions, and seek advice from peers, fostering a collaborative learning environment.

Another key aspect of empowering non-technical users is providing them with the ability to customize applications to meet specific business needs. Low-code and no-code platforms typically offer a wide range of customization options, from adjusting the layout and appearance of the user interface to defining the logic that governs how the application functions. This flexibility allows non-technical users to create applications that are tailored to their unique requirements, whether they are building a simple data-entry form or a more complex workflow automation tool. Additionally, users can define business rules and logic using visual tools, making it easy to set up triggers, automate processes, and create dynamic behaviors without having to rely on a developer. For example, a sales manager could use a no-code platform to create an automated lead assignment system that assigns leads to the appropriate sales representatives based on predefined criteria, such as region or industry.

Integration with existing systems is another essential feature of low-code and no-code platforms that helps empower non-technical users. In many organizations, applications must interact with a variety of systems, such as customer relationship management (CRM) platforms, databases, or third-party services. Low-code and no-code platforms make it easy to integrate these systems by offering pre-built connectors and APIs. Non-technical users can simply configure these integrations using visual tools, allowing data to flow seamlessly between applications without the need for custom code. For example, a marketing team can integrate a low-code application with their CRM system to pull customer data directly into their marketing campaigns, enabling more personalized and targeted communication with customers. These integrations help users build more powerful applications that interact with the broader ecosystem of tools and services used within their organization.

Low-code and no-code tools also enable non-technical users to automate tasks and workflows that would otherwise be manual. Workflow automation is one of the most powerful features of these platforms, as it allows users to create applications that automate repetitive tasks, such as data entry, approvals, or notifications. Non-technical users can design these workflows using visual tools that define the steps involved, the conditions for triggering each step, and the actions to take at each stage. For example, an HR department could use a low-code platform to automate the onboarding process for new employees, sending automated emails, assigning tasks to the relevant team members, and updating records in the company's HR system. By automating these processes, businesses can save time, reduce errors, and improve overall efficiency.

To ensure that non-technical users are fully empowered, low-code and no-code platforms must also provide tools for testing, debugging, and refining applications. Most of these platforms come with built-in testing environments that allow users to test their applications before they are deployed. These testing tools enable users to simulate different scenarios, identify issues, and make adjustments in real time. Additionally, many platforms provide analytics and reporting tools that allow users to monitor the performance of their applications once they are deployed. By giving non-technical users the tools to track usage, identify issues, and make improvements, low-code and no-code platforms enable continuous optimization of applications, ensuring that they remain effective as business needs evolve.

Security is a critical concern for any application, and low-code and no-code platforms provide non-technical users with tools to ensure that their applications are secure. These platforms typically offer built-in security features, such as role-based access control, data encryption, and user authentication. Non-technical users can configure these security features through the platform's interface, ensuring that only authorized individuals can access sensitive information or perform specific actions within the application. This level of security is essential for ensuring compliance with data protection regulations and protecting sensitive business data from unauthorized access.

Ultimately, empowering non-technical users with low-code and no-code tools allows businesses to tap into the creativity, expertise, and insights of their teams. By enabling business users to create custom applications, automate processes, and integrate systems without relying on developers, these platforms foster a culture of innovation and agility. The ability to build and iterate on applications quickly not only improves efficiency but also helps organizations stay competitive in an increasingly digital world. Low-code and no-code tools are not just about making app development easier—they are about empowering users to take control of their technology needs and drive meaningful change within their organizations.

The Impact of Low-Code/No-Code on IT Departments

In recent years, low-code and no-code platforms have gained significant traction across industries, offering businesses the ability to develop applications quickly and efficiently without extensive coding knowledge. These platforms enable non-technical users to build, customize, and deploy applications, streamlining processes and fostering innovation. While this shift has been empowering for business users, it has also had a considerable impact on IT departments. The rise of low-code and no-code tools has fundamentally altered the role of IT teams, influencing their workflows, responsibilities, and relationships with other departments.

For IT departments, the proliferation of low-code and no-code platforms presents both challenges and opportunities. One of the most significant ways these platforms affect IT teams is by reducing their involvement in the day-to-day development of business applications. Traditionally, IT departments have been responsible for all aspects of application development, from gathering requirements and writing code to testing, deploying, and maintaining systems. However, with low-code and no-code tools, business users can now take on many of these responsibilities, building applications and automating processes without requiring extensive IT resources. This shift allows IT departments to focus on higher-level tasks such as infrastructure management, security, and complex custom development, while business users take on the task of developing solutions tailored to their specific needs.

While low-code and no-code platforms enable business users to develop applications independently, they also place a new burden on IT departments in terms of governance, security, and integration. As more business units create their own applications, there is a growing need for IT teams to ensure that these applications comply with organizational standards and security protocols. IT departments must establish frameworks and guidelines to govern the use of low-code and no-code platforms, ensuring that applications are built with security, scalability, and maintainability in mind. Without proper governance, there is a risk that business users might create applications that are inefficient, insecure, or incompatible with existing systems. IT teams must also monitor the integration of these applications with legacy systems and third-party services, ensuring smooth data flows and preventing integration issues that could disrupt operations.

Low-code and no-code platforms often allow for rapid prototyping and deployment, which can be highly beneficial for businesses looking to accelerate innovation and respond to market demands. However, this speed of development can lead to challenges for IT departments tasked with ensuring that these applications are reliable and perform well under varying levels of load. IT teams must establish testing protocols to evaluate applications built on these platforms, ensuring that they meet performance standards and function correctly across different devices and environments. In some cases, IT departments may need to step in to provide technical support or to troubleshoot issues that arise with applications developed by non-technical users. While low-code and no-code platforms reduce the development time for business users, they may require IT teams to provide more oversight and intervention to maintain application quality.

Another impact of low-code and no-code platforms on IT departments is the need for upskilling. While these platforms are designed to make application development more accessible, they still require users to understand key concepts such as data management, workflows, and integration. As business users take on more responsibility for building applications, IT departments need to ensure that these users have the necessary training and resources to use these platforms effectively. In some cases, IT teams may need to provide training on best practices, security measures, and integration techniques to ensure that business users are not just building functional applications but also following organizational guidelines and industry standards. This shift in responsibility can lead to greater collaboration between business and IT teams, as both sides work together to ensure that applications are built and deployed correctly.

The growing use of low-code and no-code platforms also raises concerns about data privacy and compliance. As business users create applications that handle sensitive data, IT departments must ensure that these applications adhere to privacy regulations such as GDPR, HIPAA, or PCI-DSS. These platforms often include built-in security features such as user authentication, encryption, and access controls, but it is still up to IT teams to ensure that these features are properly configured and implemented. Additionally, IT departments must monitor the usage of sensitive data across applications, ensuring that business users do not inadvertently expose or mishandle information. This ongoing oversight is essential to maintaining data security and compliance, particularly as organizations face increasing scrutiny from regulators and customers.

While low-code and no-code platforms provide business users with the tools to build applications quickly, IT departments still play a crucial role in managing the underlying infrastructure. IT teams are responsible for ensuring that the platforms themselves are stable, scalable, and secure, and that they can support the growing needs of the organization. As businesses increase their use of these platforms, IT departments must ensure that they have the necessary resources, such as cloud infrastructure, storage, and processing power, to support the growing number of applications being developed. IT teams also need to manage access to the platforms, ensuring that only authorized users can create, modify, or deploy applications. This level of control is necessary to maintain the integrity of the development environment and prevent unauthorized changes that could negatively impact the business.

Despite these challenges, the rise of low-code and no-code platforms presents significant opportunities for IT departments to evolve and expand their roles within organizations. Rather than being bogged down in the development of every business application, IT teams can focus on strategic initiatives that drive innovation, such as building custom solutions, managing enterprise-wide integrations, and enhancing the organization's technology stack. By empowering business users to build their own applications, IT departments can shift their focus from day-to-day development to more high-level activities, enabling them to better align technology with overall business goals.

Furthermore, low-code and no-code platforms allow IT departments to drive digital transformation in a way that is both scalable and cost-effective. As more applications are developed across the organization, IT teams can help standardize processes, implement security protocols, and ensure that applications integrate seamlessly with existing systems. This helps prevent fragmentation and ensures that the organization can maintain a cohesive technology infrastructure. By enabling rapid application development and deployment, low-code and no-code platforms can help IT departments respond more quickly to business needs, supporting the organization's overall digital transformation efforts.

Ultimately, low-code and no-code platforms are reshaping the role of IT departments. While they reduce the need for IT teams to be involved in every aspect of application development, they also require IT to take on new responsibilities related to governance, security, and integration. These platforms present an opportunity for IT departments to shift from traditional development roles to more strategic, oversight-focused roles, enabling them to drive innovation and support digital transformation across the organization. By adapting to these changes and embracing low-code and no-code platforms, IT departments can play a central role in helping businesses thrive in an increasingly digital world.

The Future of Low-Code/No-Code Platforms

Low-code and no-code platforms have already made significant strides in transforming the way applications are developed, enabling non-technical users to build functional solutions with minimal coding knowledge. These platforms have allowed businesses to rapidly prototype, create custom applications, and automate workflows without waiting for developers to write lines of code. As these platforms continue to evolve, their impact on business operations, innovation, and the technology landscape will only grow. The future of low-code and no-code platforms holds immense potential, driven by advancements in artificial intelligence (AI), machine learning (ML), cloud computing, and evolving business needs. These platforms are expected to become even more powerful, user-friendly, and integrated into the broader digital ecosystem, reshaping how organizations approach software development.

The future of low-code and no-code platforms will likely see the continued democratization of application development. As businesses realize the value of empowering non-technical users to create their own applications, these platforms will become even more accessible and intuitive. The visual design interfaces that currently define low-code and no-code platforms will become more advanced, offering greater customization options and more sophisticated design capabilities. Users will be able to create highly personalized and dynamic applications without needing deep technical skills, leading to an explosion of custom solutions tailored to specific business needs. This will enable business users from various departments—marketing, finance, HR, and operations—to not only build applications but also integrate these solutions more deeply into their day-to-day workflows, all without relying on IT teams for each change.

One of the key developments in the future of low-code/no-code platforms is the incorporation of artificial intelligence and machine learning capabilities. AI and ML are already influencing many areas of business, from automation to predictive analytics, and their integration into low-code and no-code platforms will allow users to build smarter, more dynamic applications. These technologies could simplify the process of designing complex workflows, automating decision-making processes, or even providing real-time insights into application performance. For instance, AI-powered tools could analyze the data inputs and outputs of an application, suggesting improvements or automatically optimizing the workflow based on historical data. Machine learning models could also be easily integrated into applications to enhance their functionality, such as creating recommendation engines or detecting anomalies in real-time. As AI and ML continue to develop, low-code and no-code platforms will become increasingly capable of delivering advanced solutions without requiring deep expertise from the user.

Another important trend in the future of low-code and no-code platforms is the increased focus on cloud-native development. As more businesses move their operations to the cloud, low-code and no-code platforms will become even more integrated with cloud environments, allowing for seamless scalability and performance optimization. Cloud-based platforms offer the flexibility to scale applications quickly as demand increases, and low-code/no-code platforms will take full advantage of this. With built-in cloud integrations, users will be able to build applications that automatically scale to accommodate more users, handle larger data volumes, and adapt to changing business needs. This will allow businesses to build applications that can grow with them, without the need for manual intervention or complex infrastructure management. Additionally, cloud-native applications will be easier to maintain and update, as low-code/no-code platforms will automatically push updates and fixes, ensuring that businesses always have access to the latest features and security improvements.

The future of low-code and no-code platforms will also likely involve more robust integration capabilities. Currently, many platforms offer integrations with popular third-party applications and services, but as businesses continue to use a wider range of tools, the demand for deeper, more sophisticated integrations will grow. Future platforms will likely provide a broader set of connectors, allowing users to integrate with even more enterprise systems, cloud services, and data sources. This will further empower business users to build applications that work seamlessly with existing systems, eliminating the need for manual data entry or complex integrations. Advanced API management capabilities will also become a key feature, enabling users to configure, manage, and secure APIs more easily. This will create a more connected ecosystem of applications that can be easily customized and adapted to meet changing business requirements.

As low-code and no-code platforms become more powerful and feature-rich, there will also be a shift in how businesses approach governance, security, and compliance. With more business users building applications, it will be essential to have strong frameworks in place to ensure that these applications adhere to company policies, security standards, and regulatory requirements. Future low-code/no-code platforms will likely incorporate advanced security features, such as more granular user access controls, automated security monitoring, and built-in compliance tools. These platforms will ensure that non-technical users can build applications that are secure and compliant, while still maintaining the flexibility and agility that businesses need. IT departments will continue to play a crucial role in overseeing these platforms, ensuring that they are used correctly and securely, while enabling business users to take the lead in application development.

The evolving role of IT departments will also shape the future of low-code and no-code platforms. As these platforms empower business users to create and maintain applications, IT departments will need to shift their focus from traditional software development to providing oversight, support, and strategic direction. IT teams will be responsible for ensuring that applications built on these platforms are secure, scalable, and aligned with the company's technology infrastructure. Rather than being bogged down by routine development tasks, IT departments will focus on more complex, high-value projects such as custom development, enterprise integration, and system architecture. This will foster closer collaboration between business and IT teams, as both sides work together to ensure that low-code/no-code solutions meet business needs while adhering to security and governance standards.

In the future, low-code and no-code platforms will likely become even more specialized, catering to the specific needs of different industries and use cases. While these platforms are already versatile, offering solutions for a wide range of applications from internal workflow automation to customer-facing mobile apps, there will likely be platforms tailored to the unique requirements of sectors like healthcare, finance, and manufacturing. Industry-specific platforms will provide pre-built templates, workflows, and integrations that address common challenges and regulatory requirements within each sector. This will make it even easier for businesses in these industries to build applications that are customized to their needs while still benefiting from the speed and simplicity of low-code/no-code development.

The future of low-code and no-code platforms is bright, with a wealth of opportunities to accelerate digital transformation, foster innovation, and enable businesses to create customized solutions quickly and efficiently. As these platforms continue to evolve, they will become even more user-friendly, powerful, and integrated into the broader technological ecosystem. Business users will increasingly be able to create sophisticated applications that meet their unique needs, while IT departments will shift towards providing strategic oversight and guidance. With the ongoing advancements in AI, machine learning, cloud computing, and integration capabilities, low-code and no-code platforms will play a central role in the future of software development, empowering organizations to innovate faster and more effectively than ever before.

Low-Code/No-Code Development in the Cloud

The integration of low-code and no-code development platforms with cloud technologies has revolutionized the way businesses approach application development. Cloud computing has already transformed many aspects of IT infrastructure, enabling organizations to scale resources on demand, improve collaboration, and reduce costs. When combined with the accessibility and simplicity of low-code and no-code platforms, the result is an incredibly powerful solution for businesses looking to rapidly build and deploy applications with minimal coding expertise. The synergy between cloud technologies and low-code/no-code platforms not only accelerates the application development process but also enhances flexibility, scalability, and innovation across organizations.

One of the main advantages of using low-code and no-code development in the cloud is the ability to quickly deploy and scale applications. Traditionally, businesses had to invest heavily in on-premises infrastructure to host and maintain applications, requiring specialized IT resources for installation, configuration, and scaling. Cloud-based low-code and no-code platforms eliminate these barriers by hosting applications in the cloud, allowing businesses to deploy them instantly without worrying about hardware, servers, or data storage. This cloud infrastructure ensures that applications can scale easily to accommodate increasing user loads, expanding data, or growing business demands. For instance, an organization may start by developing an internal workflow automation tool for a small team and later scale it to accommodate thousands of users across different regions as the business grows, all without needing to make significant changes to the underlying infrastructure.

The cloud-based nature of low-code and no-code platforms also enhances collaboration between teams. In a traditional development environment, collaboration often required teams to be in close proximity, with constant communication between developers, designers, and business users. Cloud-based platforms remove this barrier by providing centralized access to applications and development environments, allowing users to collaborate in real-time from different locations. This is particularly valuable for organizations with distributed teams or those working in remote or hybrid environments. Cloud-based low-code/no-code platforms provide a shared space where multiple users can simultaneously contribute to the development of applications, review changes, and provide feedback without the need for physical meetings or complex version control systems. This collaborative development environment fosters faster decision-making and enables quicker iterations on application prototypes and final products.

Another significant advantage of cloud-based low-code and no-code platforms is their accessibility. With traditional software development, businesses often need to rely on specialized developers to build custom applications, which can be time-consuming and costly. Cloud-based platforms, on the other hand, allow business users who may not have technical expertise to develop their own applications. Using a visual interface, business users can design applications by dragging and dropping components, defining workflows, and integrating data sources without writing code. This ease of use allows departments such as marketing, finance, HR, and customer service to create tailored solutions that directly meet their needs, without relying on IT teams for every minor change or request. With cloud-based tools, users can access the development environment from anywhere with an internet connection, making it easier to manage applications on the go and respond to evolving business requirements in real time.

The flexibility and integration capabilities of cloud-based low-code/no-code platforms are also key factors in their success. In a cloud environment, these platforms can seamlessly integrate with other cloud-based services, tools, and data sources. Many low-code/no-code platforms offer pre-built connectors for popular cloud services like Google Cloud, AWS, Microsoft Azure, Salesforce, and more. This makes it easy to integrate applications with existing cloud-based tools, whether it's pulling customer data from a CRM system, interacting with cloud storage, or automating workflows using cloud-based messaging services. Additionally, cloud-based platforms allow for API integrations, enabling businesses to connect their low-code/no-code applications to other third-party services or on-premises systems. This level of integration makes cloud-based low-code/no-code platforms incredibly versatile, allowing businesses to create complex, interconnected applications without needing to build custom integrations from scratch.

Cloud-based low-code and no-code platforms also offer significant advantages in terms of maintenance and updates. Traditionally, updating applications and managing infrastructure required significant time and resources, as IT teams had to manually deploy patches, upgrades, and bug fixes. In a cloud environment, low-code/no-code platforms handle much of the maintenance automatically, ensuring that applications are always up to date with the latest features, security patches, and performance improvements. This eliminates the need for manual intervention, reducing downtime and ensuring that applications continue to operate smoothly as new features or fixes are rolled out. Furthermore, since the applications are hosted in the cloud, businesses do not need to worry about the underlying hardware or server infrastructure, as these are managed by the platform provider. This allows businesses to focus on innovation and application development rather than the complexities of system maintenance.

Security is another critical consideration when deploying applications in the cloud, and low-code/no-code platforms have made significant strides in ensuring that applications built on their platforms are secure. Cloud providers typically implement robust security measures, including data encryption, multi-factor authentication, and network protection. Low-code and no-code platforms built on these cloud environments inherit these security features, ensuring that the applications built by business users meet high standards of security. Additionally, many platforms provide built-in access control mechanisms, enabling businesses to define who can access, modify, or deploy applications. These security features help businesses comply with regulatory requirements such as GDPR, HIPAA, and PCI-DSS, which is particularly important for industries that handle sensitive customer data.

As the use of cloud-based low-code/no-code platforms increases, businesses will likely see a greater shift toward automation. Cloud infrastructure enables the use of intelligent automation tools that can help streamline development processes even further. For example, cloud-based platforms may integrate AI and machine learning models that allow applications to make data-driven decisions, automate repetitive tasks, and improve over time based on data inputs. This will lead to smarter applications that can continuously adapt to changing business conditions without requiring manual intervention. The integration of automation into low-code/no-code development will reduce operational costs, improve efficiency, and enable businesses to innovate at a faster pace.

The future of cloud-based low-code/no-code platforms is undoubtedly one of further integration, scalability, and intelligence. As businesses continue to demand faster development cycles, more customization, and greater flexibility, cloud-based tools will evolve to meet these needs. Advanced features such as real-time collaboration, automated testing, and deeper integrations with other cloud services will make these platforms even more indispensable. By lowering the barriers to development, increasing the speed of innovation, and improving collaboration across departments, low-code and no-code platforms in the cloud are set to play an even more critical role in shaping the digital transformation of businesses across industries. These platforms will empower organizations to develop powerful applications faster, allowing them to adapt to market demands and stay competitive in an ever-changing business environment.

Creating Cross-Platform Applications Without Code

In the rapidly evolving digital landscape, businesses are constantly looking for ways to expand their reach and create user-friendly applications that work across multiple platforms. Traditionally, developing cross-platform applications involved writing separate code for each platform, whether for iOS, Android, or web browsers. This approach was time-consuming, required specialized knowledge for each platform, and led to duplicated efforts. However, the advent of no-code platforms has completely transformed the development process. Today, non-technical users can create fully functional cross-platform applications without writing a single line of code, leveraging the power of visual interfaces, pre-built templates, and drag-and-drop components to build applications that work seamlessly across different devices and operating systems.

Creating cross-platform applications without code using these tools has become an accessible solution for businesses that want to develop high-quality applications but lack the technical resources or expertise to manage traditional development processes. The key advantage of no-code platforms is their simplicity. These platforms provide intuitive, visual interfaces that allow users to design user interfaces, configure workflows, and connect data sources without needing to understand programming languages. This is especially beneficial for small businesses or startups that may not have the budget to hire a team of developers but still need to create professional-grade applications that serve their customers across multiple platforms.

A fundamental aspect of creating cross-platform applications without code is the ability to design once and deploy everywhere. No-code platforms are designed to handle the complexities of cross-platform compatibility, so business users can create applications that automatically adjust to different screen sizes, operating systems, and devices. The platforms typically include templates and design elements that are optimized for various platforms, ensuring that the application functions well on mobile devices, tablets, and desktops. This eliminates the need for developers to write separate code for each platform, reducing both development time and costs. For example, a user can design a mobile app interface on the no-code platform, and the system will automatically adapt the design for web browsers or other platforms without additional work required.

These platforms provide a wide range of customizable pre-built components, such as forms, buttons, and navigation elements, that can be easily dragged and dropped into the application interface. Users can customize these components to match their brand's look and feel, adjusting colors, fonts, and layouts to create a unique, professional design. This visual approach to application development makes it possible for users without coding experience to focus on the business logic and user experience without worrying about the underlying code. As these platforms handle the technical complexities of responsive design, users can be confident that their applications will function smoothly across devices and screen sizes.

Moreover, the integration capabilities of no-code platforms allow users to connect their cross-platform applications to various data sources and external systems with minimal effort. In a traditional development environment, integrating applications with databases, third-party services, or APIs would require writing custom code for each platform. However, no-code platforms provide pre-built connectors and integrations for popular services, including cloud storage providers, CRM systems, payment gateways, and more. By simply configuring these integrations through a user-friendly interface, businesses can create cross-platform applications that seamlessly interact with external systems, whether pulling customer data from a CRM or processing payments through a payment gateway. This ease of integration enables non-technical users to build sophisticated applications that are connected to the broader digital ecosystem, without relying on developers for each new integration.

One of the greatest benefits of no-code platforms for creating cross-platform applications is the ability to quickly iterate and modify the app as business needs evolve. In the traditional development process, making changes to an app often involved a lengthy cycle of coding, testing, and debugging, with updates needing to be implemented separately for each platform. With no-code platforms, changes can be made in real-time, and those changes are automatically reflected across all platforms where the app is deployed. Whether adding new features, adjusting workflows, or updating the design, the speed and simplicity of this process allow businesses to stay agile and respond to user feedback or market shifts quickly. This rapid iteration is particularly valuable for businesses that need to adapt to the fast-changing demands of their customers.

Another significant advantage of creating cross-platform applications with no-code tools is the built-in security and compliance features these platforms often offer. Security is a critical concern when developing applications, especially for businesses that handle sensitive data, such as customer information or payment details. No-code platforms typically include robust security features, such as data encryption, role-based access control, and secure authentication mechanisms, ensuring that applications are protected from potential threats. These platforms also ensure compliance with industry regulations, such as GDPR, HIPAA, or PCI DSS, by including features designed to help businesses meet legal requirements. By using a no-code platform, businesses can create secure, compliant cross-platform applications without having to worry about building these security measures from scratch.

The accessibility of no-code platforms also extends to deployment. Once an application is built, deploying it across multiple platforms can be as simple as clicking a button. Many no-code platforms offer cloud-based hosting, allowing businesses to quickly launch their applications and make them available to users. Cloud-based platforms ensure that the application is scalable and can handle increasing traffic as the business grows. Whether deploying a mobile app to the App Store or Google Play or releasing a web application, the no-code platform manages the complexities of deployment, including server setup, hosting, and performance optimization. This streamlined deployment process ensures that businesses can launch their applications faster and without the logistical challenges that typically come with traditional app deployment.

While no-code platforms make it easier for non-technical users to create cross-platform applications, they also allow for some degree of customization and advanced functionality. For businesses with more complex needs or specific requirements, many no-code platforms offer advanced features like custom workflows, data processing rules, and integrations with external APIs. While these platforms are designed to be user-friendly, they also allow users to extend the app's functionality through low-code options, where users can write small amounts of code to enhance the app's capabilities. This hybrid approach ensures that no-code platforms can accommodate both simple and more complex application requirements, providing businesses with the flexibility to meet their unique needs.

The future of cross-platform development without code is bright. As these platforms continue to evolve, they will become even more powerful, offering deeper integration capabilities, enhanced automation, and more sophisticated design tools. With advancements in artificial intelligence, machine learning, and cloud technologies, no-code platforms will enable businesses to create even more advanced applications, such as AI-powered tools, real-time data processing systems, and sophisticated automation workflows—all without the need for traditional coding expertise. As these platforms become more refined, businesses will be able to create increasingly complex and feature-rich cross-platform applications that drive innovation and deliver exceptional user experiences.

Creating cross-platform applications without code is not only a practical solution for businesses today but also a powerful tool for innovation and agility in the future. No-code platforms enable businesses to take control of their application development process, building solutions that meet their specific needs while remaining flexible and scalable. As these tools continue to evolve, the possibilities for businesses to rapidly develop and deploy cross-platform applications will only expand, offering a more streamlined and efficient way to deliver value to customers and stakeholders.

Customizing Low-Code/No-Code Applications to Fit Business Needs

In the dynamic world of business, companies are constantly seeking ways to streamline operations, increase efficiency, and stay ahead of competitors. One of the most powerful tools businesses can leverage to achieve these goals is low-code and no-code platforms. These platforms enable non-technical users to create applications quickly and efficiently, but their real value lies in the ability to customize those applications to meet specific business needs. Customizing low-code and no-code applications allows businesses to tailor solutions that align with their unique workflows, processes, and objectives without relying heavily on IT resources. The ability to build custom applications that fit the specific needs of a business, all while maintaining agility and reducing costs, is a game-changer in today's fast-paced business environment.

Customizing applications built on low-code and no-code platforms begins with understanding the fundamental needs of the business.

Whether it's automating internal processes, enhancing customer engagement, or integrating various business systems, the first step in customization is identifying the exact requirements of the business. These platforms provide a range of pre-built templates and components that serve as starting points, but the true power lies in the ability to adapt these templates to suit particular workflows and business goals. For instance, a marketing team might use a no-code platform to develop a customer relationship management (CRM) system that fits their unique sales pipeline, customer touchpoints, and marketing campaigns. The flexibility of these platforms allows the marketing team to create custom fields, workflows, and data structures that match the team's specific requirements.

Once the business needs have been identified, customization continues by modifying the user interface (UI) and user experience (UX) to align with the company's branding and desired interactions. Low-code and no-code platforms offer a variety of visual design tools, enabling users to drag and drop components such as buttons, forms, and data fields onto the application interface. These components can be customized to reflect the company's branding, from adjusting color schemes and fonts to adding custom logos and icons. Customizing the UI ensures that the application provides a seamless and consistent experience for users while reinforcing the company's identity. Additionally, customization allows businesses to prioritize the most important features or information for their users, ensuring that the application serves its intended purpose effectively.

One of the most significant advantages of low-code and no-code platforms is their ability to adapt to changing business requirements. As companies grow or pivot their strategies, they often need to update or change their software solutions to meet new demands. Low-code and no-code platforms make it easy to modify applications quickly in response to these changes. For example, if a company decides to expand into a new market and needs to capture additional customer data, the application can be updated to include new fields or workflows without requiring a complete rebuild. These platforms offer the flexibility to make such changes in real-time, ensuring that businesses can respond to new opportunities or challenges without the lengthy development cycles associated with traditional software development.

Another key area where customization plays a crucial role is in workflow automation. Low-code and no-code platforms excel at automating repetitive tasks, and businesses can easily customize these automation processes to fit their specific needs. Workflow automation can range from simple tasks, like sending an email when a form is submitted, to more complex processes, like managing multi-step approval systems or inventory tracking. These platforms allow users to define business rules and triggers visually, making it possible to automate tasks across different systems and departments. For instance, a company might use a no-code platform to create a system that automatically routes support tickets to the appropriate department based on the type of inquiry, or sends reminders to sales representatives when it's time to follow up with a client. This level of customization reduces the need for manual intervention, increases productivity, and ensures consistency across the business.

In addition to user interface and workflow customization, low-code and no-code platforms also allow businesses to customize the data structures and logic that power their applications. Businesses can define custom data models to capture the information that matters most to them, whether it's customer details, sales performance, or project status. These platforms provide an easy way to create custom fields, tables, and relationships between data sets, ensuring that the application supports the business's specific data management needs. Moreover, businesses can implement logic to control how data is processed and displayed within the application, such as creating conditional workflows that adjust based on user inputs or integrating advanced calculations to analyze data in real-time. This flexibility ensures that applications are not only visually aligned with business needs but are also capable of performing complex functions that drive decision-making and performance.

One of the standout features of low-code and no-code platforms is their ability to integrate with external systems and services, which is essential for creating customized applications that fit into the broader technology ecosystem of the business. Many low-code platforms provide pre-built connectors for popular third-party services, such as customer relationship management (CRM) systems, email marketing platforms, or payment gateways. These integrations enable businesses to bring in data from multiple sources, automate processes, and create a more cohesive system across the organization. For instance, a retail business could integrate an e-commerce platform with an inventory management system to automatically update stock levels in real-time. Customizing the integration of these tools ensures that businesses can connect their low-code applications with their existing infrastructure, enhancing their overall functionality and reducing manual work.

The security and compliance features offered by low-code and no-code platforms also allow for customized access controls and data protection measures. Businesses often need to ensure that only authorized users have access to certain features or data within the application. Low-code and no-code platforms provide role-based access controls (RBAC), allowing businesses to define different access levels for users based on their roles within the organization. For example, a manager may have full access to modify workflows and view all customer data, while a team member may only have access to their assigned tasks or data. Customizing these access controls ensures that the application is secure, compliant with relevant regulations, and protects sensitive information. Additionally, businesses can implement data encryption, multi-factor authentication (MFA), and other security measures to safeguard their applications from potential threats.

The ability to customize applications built on low-code and no-code platforms also opens the door to continuous improvement. Once an application is deployed, businesses can continue to tweak and optimize it based on user feedback and changing business needs. Unlike traditional development, which often involves long cycles of coding, testing, and deployment, low-code and no-code platforms allow businesses to make incremental updates and improvements without disrupting operations. Whether it's adding new features, adjusting workflows, or enhancing the user experience, the customization possibilities are vast and can be implemented with minimal downtime.

The flexibility and ease of customization in low-code and no-code platforms have transformed the way businesses approach application development. By empowering business users to design, modify, and optimize applications that directly address their unique needs, these platforms have enabled companies to create highly personalized solutions quickly and cost-effectively. As businesses continue to adapt to ever-changing market demands, the ability to customize applications without relying on extensive coding expertise will become an essential part of staying competitive and driving innovation. Low-code and no-code platforms have paved the way for a new era of application development, where business users can take control of their solutions and create applications that truly reflect the needs of their organization.

Integrating Low-Code/No-Code Apps with Legacy Systems

The digital transformation of businesses often involves the integration of new, innovative solutions with legacy systems that have long been the backbone of organizational operations. As businesses seek to modernize their operations, they often face the challenge of connecting low-code and no-code applications with these existing systems. Legacy systems, which may include older databases, enterprise resource planning (ERP) tools, customer relationship management (CRM) platforms, and other proprietary software, can pose significant barriers to innovation. However, low-code and no-code platforms are uniquely positioned to bridge the gap between modern applications and legacy systems, offering businesses the flexibility to develop new solutions while still leveraging their existing infrastructure. By integrating low-code and no-code apps with legacy systems, organizations can enhance operational efficiency, streamline workflows, and create a more cohesive technology ecosystem without completely overhauling their legacy systems.

One of the primary challenges when integrating low-code and no-code applications with legacy systems is that these older systems were often not designed to work with modern cloud-based applications. Many legacy systems operate in isolated environments, use outdated data formats, or lack the necessary APIs for easy integration. This can make it difficult to establish a seamless connection between new applications and legacy systems. However, low-code and no-code platforms often include pre-built connectors, integration tools, and application programming interfaces (APIs) that can facilitate the integration process. These platforms allow businesses to build bridges between modern applications and older systems by creating data pipelines, ensuring that information can flow freely between systems, without the need for extensive coding. These tools can be configured through simple visual interfaces, enabling non-technical users to handle the integration process without requiring the expertise of specialized developers.

One common approach to integrating low-code and no-code apps with legacy systems is the use of middleware. Middleware acts as an intermediary layer that sits between the modern application and the legacy system, facilitating communication between the two. This can be especially useful when the legacy system lacks the capability to expose its data through modern API protocols, or when there is a need to connect multiple disparate systems. Middleware tools can convert data from the older system's format into something the low-code or no-code app can understand, and vice versa. These tools can be configured within the low-code platform, allowing businesses to integrate legacy systems with minimal effort. Middleware not only helps connect systems but can also enhance data security, ensuring that sensitive information is handled appropriately during the integration process.

In many cases, low-code and no-code platforms come equipped with a wide range of pre-built integrations that simplify the process of connecting to legacy systems. For example, platforms like Microsoft Power Apps or Salesforce allow users to connect their applications to older databases, CRM systems, or ERP tools. These pre-built connectors provide a direct link between the modern application and the legacy system, eliminating the need for complex custom coding. These platforms often support common data exchange protocols such as REST, SOAP, and OData, allowing them to interface with legacy systems regardless of their age or underlying technology. The use of pre-built integrations reduces the time and cost associated with building custom integration solutions, allowing businesses to focus on creating value-driven applications rather than dealing with the intricacies of legacy system connections.

Another method of integrating low-code and no-code applications with legacy systems is through the use of batch processing and data synchronization. In cases where real-time integration is not feasible, batch processing allows businesses to periodically transfer data between the modern application and the legacy system. This approach can be especially useful when dealing with systems that cannot support real-time data exchange or when the volume of data is too large to process instantaneously. Low-code platforms allow businesses to automate the process of synchronizing data between legacy systems and modern applications, ensuring that the data is consistently up to date without requiring manual intervention. For example, a business could use a no-code platform to create an inventory management app that pulls data from an old inventory system once a day, keeping the two systems in sync while minimizing the load on both platforms.

The ability to integrate low-code and no-code applications with legacy systems can significantly enhance business operations by enabling organizations to retain valuable legacy investments while still adopting modern solutions. For instance, a company that relies on a legacy CRM system may use a low-code platform to create a custom sales management application that pulls data from the CRM, allowing sales teams to access the most up-to-date customer information in a more user-friendly interface. This approach not only modernizes the sales process but also ensures that valuable customer data remains accessible and consistent across the business. By integrating the new application with the legacy system, the organization avoids duplicating data entry and reduces the risk of data silos, where information is fragmented across multiple systems.

Additionally, low-code and no-code platforms can be used to enhance the functionality of legacy systems by adding new features that were not available in the original software. For example, an organization might use a low-code platform to build a mobile app that interfaces with a legacy inventory management system, providing warehouse employees with real-time updates on stock levels, order statuses, and product locations. While the legacy system may not have been designed with mobile access in mind, the low-code platform enables the organization to create a solution that fills this gap, extending the capabilities of the existing system. This ability to enhance legacy systems without replacing them is a significant advantage for businesses looking to modernize their operations in a cost-effective manner.

The integration of low-code and no-code applications with legacy systems can also improve decision-making by providing a unified view of data across platforms. Often, businesses struggle to obtain comprehensive insights because critical data is spread across multiple legacy systems. By connecting these systems to modern applications, businesses can consolidate their data into a single dashboard or reporting tool, allowing decision-makers to access real-time insights and make informed choices. Low-code platforms offer a simple way to create custom dashboards that pull data from legacy systems, presenting it in an easy-to-understand format. These dashboards can be tailored to show key performance indicators (KPIs), trends, and other business-critical data, ensuring that decision-makers have the information they need to drive the business forward.

Finally, integrating low-code and no-code applications with legacy systems enhances organizational agility. In today's business environment, companies need to be able to pivot quickly in response to changing market conditions or customer needs. Low-code platforms allow businesses to develop and deploy new applications rapidly, while still ensuring that these applications can work with existing systems. This flexibility allows businesses to respond faster to emerging opportunities or challenges, without being hindered by outdated technology or complex integration processes. By creating custom applications that leverage legacy systems and modern tools, organizations can create a more adaptable and responsive technology ecosystem.

The integration of low-code and no-code applications with legacy systems is not only possible but also beneficial for organizations looking to modernize their operations. These platforms allow businesses to bridge the gap between old and new technologies, enabling them to maximize the value of their legacy systems while benefiting from the speed, flexibility, and innovation of modern application development. Through pre-built connectors, middleware, batch processing, and custom integrations, low-code and no-code platforms enable businesses to create connected, efficient, and scalable solutions that meet their evolving needs.

Performance Optimization in Low-Code/No-Code Applications

As businesses increasingly turn to low-code and no-code platforms to streamline application development, the need for performance optimization becomes more critical. These platforms empower business users, often without technical backgrounds, to create functional applications quickly, but the inherent complexity of applications and the variety of environments in which they operate require careful attention to performance. While these platforms simplify the development process by providing pre-built components and visual interfaces, the efficiency and effectiveness of the resulting applications are largely determined by how well they are optimized for performance. Ensuring that low-code and no-code applications perform at their best is crucial for delivering a seamless user experience, reducing operational bottlenecks, and maintaining scalability as the application grows.

Performance optimization in low-code and no-code applications starts with understanding the factors that impact their efficiency. These applications are typically built using visual tools, which can sometimes result in code that is not as optimized as hand-written code. While low-code/no-code platforms abstract away the complexity of coding, the generated code may not be as efficient as traditional software written by experienced developers. This means that performance issues such as slow load times, poor responsiveness, and inefficiencies in data processing can arise, particularly as the application scales. Therefore, one of the first steps in optimizing performance is for business users to design their applications with scalability in mind, avoiding overly complex workflows and reducing unnecessary elements that could negatively affect speed.

One of the key areas where performance optimization is essential in low-code/no-code applications is data management. Applications that rely heavily on data—whether for customer interactions, inventory tracking, or reporting—must handle large volumes of information efficiently. Low-code and no-code platforms often allow users to connect applications to databases or external data sources, which can introduce performance bottlenecks if not managed properly. Poorly designed data models or inefficient queries can lead to slow response times and increased load on the system, particularly when multiple users are accessing the application simultaneously. To optimize data performance, it is essential to carefully design data models, ensuring that tables are normalized and indexed appropriately. Additionally, reducing the number of API calls or queries that are made during each user interaction can minimize the load on the system and improve response times.

Another important consideration in performance optimization is minimizing the amount of data processed at any given time. Low-code and no-code platforms often provide users with easy ways to display data in tables, charts, or grids, but displaying too much data at once can overwhelm the system and lead to slow load times. For example, displaying thousands of rows in a table on a single page can lead to performance issues, especially on mobile devices. To address this, developers can optimize applications by using techniques like pagination, lazy loading, or infinite scrolling, which load data incrementally as the user interacts with the application. These techniques ensure that only a small subset of data is loaded initially, reducing the initial load time and improving the responsiveness of the application.

Reducing the number of third-party integrations and API calls is also a key aspect of performance optimization. Many low-code and no-code platforms allow users to integrate with external systems such as CRMs, payment gateways, and cloud storage services. While these integrations add functionality to the application, they can also introduce performance issues if not optimized. Each API call or external request adds latency to the application, so minimizing unnecessary calls and ensuring that data is retrieved in the most efficient manner possible is essential. For example, instead of making separate API calls to retrieve each piece of data, developers can batch requests into a single call, reducing the time spent waiting for external systems to respond. Additionally, caching frequently accessed data can significantly reduce the need for repeated API calls, further improving the application's performance.

In addition to optimizing data management and integrations, user interface (UI) design plays a critical role in performance. The complexity of the UI can directly affect how quickly an application loads and responds to user interactions. Low-code and no-code platforms provide drag-and-drop tools for designing user interfaces, but it is important to keep the design simple and focused on the most important functionality. Overly complex UIs with too many elements can slow down the application, especially on mobile devices or browsers with limited resources. To optimize performance, designers should minimize the number of images, scripts, and animations used in the UI and ensure that the application is responsive across different screen sizes and devices. By focusing on a clean, simple design that prioritizes user experience, businesses can improve the overall performance of their low-code/no-code applications.

Another critical aspect of performance optimization is testing and monitoring the application throughout its lifecycle. Performance issues may not always be apparent during development but can become evident as more users interact with the application or as the complexity of the data increases. Therefore, it is essential to continuously test and monitor the performance of the application to identify and resolve any potential bottlenecks. Many low-code and no-code platforms provide built-in tools for testing and monitoring, allowing businesses to evaluate how their applications perform under different conditions. These tools can simulate high traffic, monitor response times, and provide insights into resource usage, helping businesses pinpoint areas that need optimization. By regularly testing and monitoring the application, businesses can ensure that it remains responsive and scalable as it evolves.

As low-code and no-code platforms evolve, they will likely offer even more advanced performance optimization features, such as automated load balancing, optimized data storage solutions, and more powerful back-end integrations. These features will help businesses further enhance the performance of their applications while maintaining the flexibility and ease of use that low-code/no-code platforms provide. Additionally, with the increasing adoption of cloud-based infrastructure, many low-code and no-code platforms will leverage the scalability and performance capabilities of the cloud to automatically scale resources based on demand. This means that applications can dynamically adjust to handle varying traffic levels, ensuring consistent performance even during peak usage times.

One of the challenges with low-code and no-code platforms is that they often abstract away much of the technical detail, which can make it difficult for business users to fully understand the performance implications of their design decisions. However, as these platforms become more sophisticated, they are likely to include more advanced performance management tools, enabling users to fine-tune their applications for optimal performance. These tools might include automated performance suggestions, data analysis features, and optimization guidelines, allowing non-technical users to make informed decisions about how to improve the performance of their applications.

Low-code and no-code platforms have the potential to drive significant improvements in efficiency, productivity, and agility within organizations. However, for these applications to deliver on their promise, businesses must prioritize performance optimization throughout the development process. By focusing on efficient data management, minimizing unnecessary integrations, simplifying the user interface, and continuously testing and monitoring applications, organizations can ensure that their low-code and no-code solutions perform at their best. As the demand for faster, more responsive applications continues to grow, performance optimization will remain a critical factor in the success of low-code and no-code platforms. With the right strategies and tools in place, businesses can create applications that are not only easy to build but also highly performant, scalable, and capable of meeting the demands of modern users.

Handling Data Privacy and Protection in Low-Code/No-Code Development

As businesses increasingly turn to low-code and no-code platforms to develop applications quickly and efficiently, one of the most critical concerns that arise is data privacy and protection. These platforms enable users with minimal technical expertise to design and deploy applications, but they also come with the responsibility of handling sensitive data securely. The rapid growth of digital platforms, along with stricter data protection regulations, has made it essential for organizations to ensure that their applications comply with privacy laws and safeguard user information. Given that low-code and no-code platforms often simplify many aspects of application development, it is important to understand the complexities of data privacy and protection in the context of these platforms and how to mitigate risks effectively.

Data privacy and protection in low-code and no-code development involve several key considerations. First and foremost, it is essential to understand the nature of the data being handled. Personal data, such as names, addresses, contact information, and financial details, as well as sensitive data like health information or payment card details, must be treated with the highest level of care. Applications built on low-code and no-code platforms are no exception, and ensuring that these platforms provide the necessary tools to handle such data securely is crucial. Businesses must ensure that their applications are designed in a way that minimizes exposure to risks and meets the necessary legal and regulatory standards, such as the General Data Protection Regulation (GDPR) or the Health Insurance Portability and Accountability Act (HIPAA).

One of the primary concerns when using low-code and no-code platforms is the security of the data being stored and processed. These platforms typically provide cloud-based storage solutions, which offer scalability and accessibility, but also introduce potential risks in terms of data security. The cloud infrastructure underlying low-code/no-code platforms must be secure, and businesses must ensure that their applications are using robust encryption methods to protect data both in transit and at rest. Data encryption ensures that sensitive information is unreadable to unauthorized users and provides an additional layer of security when data is stored or transmitted across networks. Low-code and no-code platforms often include built-in security features, such as encryption and secure storage, but businesses must verify that these tools are configured correctly and meet the specific security requirements of their industry.

Access control is another critical component of data privacy and protection in low-code and no-code development. These platforms typically allow users to set up role-based access controls (RBAC), which define who can access certain features or data within an application.

Businesses must ensure that only authorized individuals have access to sensitive data and critical functions within the application. For example, administrators may need full access to all aspects of the application, while end users may only need access to specific data or features. Setting up granular access controls helps prevent unauthorized access and minimizes the risk of data breaches. Additionally, low-code/no-code platforms often include the ability to implement multi-factor authentication (MFA), which provides an added layer of security by requiring users to verify their identity through multiple methods, such as a password and a one-time code sent to their phone.

As businesses increasingly rely on third-party integrations to enhance the functionality of their low-code and no-code applications, it is important to consider how these integrations affect data privacy. Many low-code and no-code platforms offer integrations with external systems, such as customer relationship management (CRM) tools, payment gateways, and cloud storage services. While these integrations provide powerful functionality, they also introduce potential vulnerabilities, especially when data is being transmitted between multiple systems. To mitigate these risks, businesses should carefully review the security practices and privacy policies of third-party vendors to ensure that they align with their own data protection standards. Secure application programming interfaces (APIs) are essential for ensuring that data is exchanged between systems securely. By implementing secure API connections, businesses can ensure that sensitive data is protected as it moves between applications.

Another critical aspect of data privacy in low-code and no-code development is compliance with data protection regulations. Different regions have different laws governing how personal data must be handled, and it is essential for businesses to ensure that their applications comply with these regulations. For example, GDPR mandates strict rules on how personal data should be collected, stored, and processed, as well as giving individuals the right to access, correct, and delete their data. Low-code and no-code platforms often provide tools to help businesses comply with these regulations, such as data retention policies, the ability to request consent from users, and features for managing user access to their data. However, businesses must actively ensure that these tools are configured properly and that their applications are in line with the specific requirements of the regulations they are subject to.

Data protection also requires businesses to think about how they handle and manage data after it is collected. It is not enough to simply secure data during its collection or transmission; businesses must also ensure that data is properly stored, archived, and deleted when no longer needed. Low-code and no-code platforms often include features for automating the deletion of data after a set period, or when users request it, ensuring that businesses comply with "right to be forgotten" regulations under laws like GDPR. Establishing clear data retention and disposal policies is an important part of maintaining data privacy and protection in the long term.

One area where low-code and no-code platforms offer significant advantages is the ability to rapidly test and iterate on applications. However, businesses must ensure that privacy and security considerations are built into the development process from the outset. During the testing phase, businesses should simulate various security threats and test the application's resilience against common vulnerabilities, such as SQL injection or cross-site scripting attacks. Low-code and no-code platforms often include built-in security testing tools that can help identify potential weaknesses, but businesses should also engage in manual security assessments or work with external experts to ensure comprehensive protection.

In addition to the technical aspects of data protection, businesses must also foster a culture of awareness around data privacy. Educating employees about best practices for handling sensitive data, setting clear internal policies for data access, and ensuring regular security audits are crucial components of maintaining strong data protection practices. Even though low-code and no-code platforms simplify many aspects of development, the responsibility for ensuring data privacy and protection still lies with the business. By implementing a culture of security, conducting regular training, and keeping up with evolving data protection laws, businesses can mitigate risks and create a secure environment for managing sensitive data.

As low-code and no-code platforms continue to grow in popularity and sophistication, their role in data privacy and protection will become even more critical. The ease of use and accessibility of these platforms make it easier for non-technical users to create powerful applications, but businesses must ensure they are equipped with the knowledge and tools to handle sensitive data responsibly. By integrating security features, following regulatory guidelines, and continuously monitoring data protection practices, organizations can leverage the full potential of low-code and no-code platforms while safeguarding the privacy of their users and maintaining compliance with industry regulations. With the right approach, businesses can create secure, user-friendly applications that empower both users and organizations alike.

Building SaaS Applications with Low-Code/No-Code Platforms

The Software as a Service (SaaS) model has become a cornerstone of modern business operations, providing scalable, accessible, and flexible solutions that can be tailored to meet the unique needs of companies across industries. However, building SaaS applications traditionally requires significant time, technical expertise, and resources, which often puts them out of reach for small businesses or organizations with limited IT infrastructure. Low-code and no-code platforms have changed this dynamic by enabling businesses to create powerful, custom SaaS applications without the need for extensive coding knowledge. These platforms offer a simplified approach to application development, empowering non-technical users to design, build, and deploy SaaS solutions that meet their specific business requirements quickly and efficiently.

The first step in building a SaaS application using low-code or no-code platforms is understanding the core functionalities that the application will need to provide. SaaS applications are designed to be accessed via the internet, usually through a subscription model, and they serve a wide range of functions, from customer relationship management (CRM) to project management, invoicing, or data analytics. Low-code and no-code platforms provide a broad range of templates and pre-built components that can be easily customized to match the specific business needs of the SaaS product. For instance, businesses can choose templates that provide basic CRM functionalities, then modify them by adding custom fields, workflows, or integrations based on their requirements. This approach allows businesses to focus on the application's core value propositions while relying on the platform to handle the underlying technical complexity.

Low-code and no-code platforms also simplify the creation of multi-tenant SaaS applications, which allow multiple customers to access the same instance of the application while keeping their data separate and secure. Building a multi-tenant application traditionally requires intricate database management and user access control configurations, which could be complex and time-consuming. However, with low-code and no-code platforms, the process is simplified. These platforms come equipped with built-in user management tools, data partitioning features, and role-based access control (RBAC), which makes it easier to define who can access specific features or data within the application. By configuring these features using the visual interface provided by the platform, businesses can rapidly build multi-tenant applications that meet security and scalability requirements without needing to write complex code.

A critical element of SaaS application development is ensuring that the application is scalable and can handle the growth of both users and data over time. Low-code and no-code platforms are built to support scalability, providing cloud-based hosting that automatically adjusts resources as the application grows. This means that businesses do not need to worry about managing the infrastructure themselves or dealing with capacity planning and server configurations. The platform automatically scales the application to accommodate more users, greater data storage, and higher processing power. By taking advantage of cloud services and the scalability built into many low-code and no-code platforms, businesses can focus on developing the application's functionality rather than worrying about managing the underlying infrastructure.

Another benefit of building SaaS applications on low-code and no-code platforms is the speed of development. Traditional SaaS application development often involves lengthy cycles of coding, testing, and debugging, which can take months or even years. With low-code and no-code platforms, the development cycle is significantly shortened.

These platforms offer drag-and-drop interfaces, visual workflow builders, and reusable components that allow business users to quickly design the user interface (UI), configure business logic, and connect data sources. This rapid development process enables businesses to get their SaaS applications to market faster, allowing them to meet customer needs and market demands more quickly.

Integrations are a critical aspect of SaaS applications, as they allow the application to connect with other tools, services, and platforms that businesses already use. Whether integrating with payment gateways, customer support systems, social media platforms, or email marketing services, low-code and no-code platforms offer pre-built connectors and integration options that make it easy to connect the SaaS application to a wide range of third-party services. Instead of writing complex code to handle these integrations, users can simply configure the connections through a visual interface, saving time and effort. Additionally, these platforms support common integration standards such as REST APIs, making it possible to connect the application to virtually any modern service with ease. These integrations not only enhance the functionality of the SaaS application but also ensure that businesses can provide a seamless experience for their customers.

User experience (UX) is one of the most important considerations when building SaaS applications. The ease of use, visual appeal, and responsiveness of the application can have a significant impact on customer satisfaction and retention. Low-code and no-code platforms offer a variety of tools for designing intuitive and engaging user interfaces without the need for a dedicated UX/UI designer. These platforms provide drag-and-drop tools for arranging UI components, customizing layouts, and applying branding elements such as logos, color schemes, and fonts. Furthermore, many low-code platforms include features for making the application responsive, ensuring that it works seamlessly across various devices, such as desktops, tablets, and smartphones. This ease of customization allows businesses to create SaaS applications that are not only functional but also deliver an outstanding user experience that encourages engagement and adoption.

Security and data privacy are critical considerations when building SaaS applications, particularly when handling sensitive customer data.

Low-code and no-code platforms offer robust security features to ensure that data is protected both during transmission and while at rest. These platforms often include encryption tools, secure authentication methods, and compliance with various data protection regulations such as GDPR, HIPAA, and PCI-DSS. Additionally, businesses can implement role-based access controls (RBAC) to restrict user access to sensitive data and functionalities, further safeguarding customer information. By leveraging these built-in security features, businesses can build secure SaaS applications without the need to design complex security protocols from scratch.

As businesses scale their SaaS applications, monitoring and maintenance become essential to ensuring continued performance, security, and customer satisfaction. Low-code and no-code platforms typically provide built-in monitoring and analytics tools that track application performance, user activity, and system health. These tools enable businesses to monitor key metrics such as server uptime, response times, user engagement, and error logs, which can help identify issues before they impact users. Furthermore, many platforms offer automated updates and patches, ensuring that the application remains up-to-date with the latest security features and functionality. This ongoing maintenance process is streamlined by the platform's built-in capabilities, allowing businesses to focus on innovation and feature development rather than manual maintenance tasks.

Building SaaS applications using low-code and no-code platforms offers many advantages, particularly in terms of speed, cost, and ease of use. These platforms simplify the development process, allowing business users to create custom applications without the need for extensive technical knowledge. By offering built-in scalability, security, integration options, and responsive design tools, low-code and no-code platforms provide everything businesses need to create powerful, secure, and scalable SaaS applications. As businesses continue to seek ways to innovate and meet customer demands, low-code and no-code platforms are becoming indispensable tools for developing SaaS solutions that drive success. The ability to rapidly prototype, iterate, and deploy SaaS applications, all while keeping costs low and development cycles short, is helping organizations across the globe enhance their digital capabilities and stay competitive in an increasingly fast-paced market.

Low-Code/No-Code for the Financial Services Industry

The financial services industry is one of the most regulated and complex sectors, requiring high levels of accuracy, security, and efficiency. Traditional methods of software development in financial institutions have often been time-consuming, costly, and resource-intensive, which can lead to delays in bringing innovative solutions to market. However, the advent of low-code and no-code platforms has begun to transform how financial services companies develop and deploy applications. These platforms enable financial institutions to rapidly create customized solutions, automate workflows, and improve operational efficiency without the need for extensive coding or reliance on large IT teams. As a result, financial services organizations are now able to respond more quickly to changing market demands, enhance customer experiences, and innovate more efficiently.

One of the key advantages of low-code and no-code platforms in the financial services industry is the speed at which applications can be developed and deployed. Traditionally, financial institutions would need to dedicate months or even years to develop new software solutions, often requiring a large team of developers, project managers, and IT specialists. With low-code and no-code platforms, the development cycle is drastically shortened. These platforms provide intuitive, drag-and-drop tools that enable business users—who may not have technical expertise—to design, build, and deploy applications in a fraction of the time. For example, a financial services company could quickly develop a custom customer portal, mobile app, or internal reporting tool tailored to its unique requirements, all without needing to hire specialized developers. This speed of development allows financial institutions to innovate more quickly and respond to customer needs in real-time, which is critical in a fast-paced and competitive industry.

In the highly regulated world of financial services, ensuring compliance with laws and regulations is of paramount importance. Financial institutions must adhere to various standards such as the General Data

Protection Regulation (GDPR), Payment Card Industry Data Security Standard (PCI DSS), and the Dodd-Frank Act, among many others. Low-code and no-code platforms have built-in features that help financial institutions manage compliance more easily. These platforms often include security features such as encryption, role-based access control, and audit trails, all of which are essential for protecting sensitive financial data. Furthermore, many of these platforms offer pre-configured templates that are designed with regulatory compliance in mind, ensuring that the applications built on these platforms meet industry standards. By utilizing low-code/no-code platforms, financial services organizations can focus on developing solutions that meet their business needs while ensuring compliance with regulatory requirements, without the need for extensive custom development.

Another important benefit of low-code and no-code platforms in the financial services sector is their ability to integrate with a wide range of existing systems and data sources. In financial institutions, there are often many disparate systems used to manage customer data, financial transactions, compliance records, and other critical information. Low-code and no-code platforms offer seamless integration with these systems, allowing data to flow smoothly between different platforms. This integration capability is especially important for financial institutions that need to connect their legacy systems with modern applications. For instance, a bank could use a low-code platform to build an application that integrates with its core banking system, customer relationship management (CRM) tools, and other financial systems, providing employees with a unified view of customer data, transactions, and account information. This integration improves efficiency by reducing the need for manual data entry and ensuring that employees have access to real-time, accurate information across all systems.

Customer experience is another critical area where low-code and no-code platforms can make a significant impact in the financial services industry. Financial institutions must provide their customers with seamless, user-friendly experiences, whether they are using mobile banking apps, managing investments, or applying for loans. With low-code and no-code platforms, financial services organizations can quickly build and customize applications that meet the specific needs of their customers. These platforms offer visual design tools that allow businesses to create responsive, intuitive interfaces without relying on specialized designers or developers. For example, a financial institution could use a no-code platform to create a personalized dashboard for each customer, allowing them to track their account balances, view recent transactions, and manage their investments—all from a single interface. By enabling businesses to create applications that are tailored to their customers' preferences, low-code and no-code platforms help financial services organizations enhance customer satisfaction, drive engagement, and build long-term relationships.

Risk management and fraud prevention are critical concerns for financial services companies. In a constantly evolving environment, financial institutions must be able to identify and mitigate potential risks in real-time. Low-code and no-code platforms can help automate many of the risk management processes, such as transaction monitoring, fraud detection, and compliance checks. By using these platforms, financial institutions can quickly develop applications that scan transactions for unusual activity, flag potential fraudulent behavior, and generate alerts for further investigation. These platforms can also automate the process of verifying customer identities, cross-referencing personal information with external databases to prevent identity theft and money laundering. Automating these processes using low-code/no-code platforms not only saves time but also reduces the likelihood of human error, which is particularly important when dealing with financial data.

Low-code and no-code platforms also play a significant role in improving internal operations within financial institutions. These platforms enable the automation of workflows, reducing the need for manual processes and ensuring that tasks are completed efficiently and accurately. For example, a bank could automate the process of onboarding new customers by creating a custom application that guides customers through the necessary steps, verifies their identity, and generates the required paperwork. Similarly, internal processes such as loan approvals, expense tracking, and document management can be streamlined using low-code and no-code tools. By automating these processes, financial institutions can reduce operational costs, improve productivity, and minimize the risk of errors or delays.

One of the challenges financial services organizations face when adopting low-code and no-code platforms is ensuring that these applications are secure and scalable. Financial institutions handle vast amounts of sensitive data, and the integrity of their applications is critical. Fortunately, many low-code/no-code platforms are built with security and scalability in mind. These platforms offer features such as cloud-based hosting, encryption, and compliance with industry standards, allowing financial institutions to build applications that are both secure and scalable. Additionally, the cloud-based nature of these platforms means that applications can easily be scaled to handle increased traffic or demand as the business grows, ensuring that the application remains responsive and reliable even as the user base expands.

Low-code and no-code platforms have the potential to revolutionize the financial services industry by enabling businesses to develop customized applications faster, reduce operational costs, and enhance customer experiences. By simplifying the development process and making it accessible to non-technical users, these platforms provide financial services organizations with the tools they need to innovate more rapidly and efficiently. Whether it's creating custom applications for customer engagement, automating risk management processes, or ensuring regulatory compliance, low-code and no-code platforms are becoming essential tools in the financial services sector. As these platforms continue to evolve and offer more advanced features, their role in shaping the future of financial services will only grow.

Low-Code/No-Code Development for Healthcare Applications

The healthcare industry has long been dependent on complex systems to manage patient data, coordinate care, and ensure compliance with strict regulations. However, as the demand for more personalized, accessible, and efficient healthcare services continues to rise, the limitations of traditional software development have become apparent. The lengthy and costly development cycles, combined with the need for specialized IT teams, have made it difficult for healthcare providers to keep up with the fast pace of innovation. Low-code and no-code development platforms have emerged as an essential tool for healthcare organizations looking to create custom applications quickly, streamline workflows, and improve patient care. These platforms empower non-technical users, such as healthcare professionals, administrators, and managers, to develop and deploy applications that meet the specific needs of their organizations without relying on developers for every change or enhancement.

One of the most significant advantages of low-code and no-code platforms in healthcare is the ability to rapidly prototype and deploy applications that meet the immediate needs of medical professionals and patients. In a field where technology must continuously evolve to meet regulatory requirements, patient needs, and industry best practices, low-code and no-code platforms allow for quick, agile development. These platforms offer visual interfaces where users can design, configure, and test applications without writing any code. This is especially beneficial in healthcare, where a hospital or clinic may need to create a patient tracking system or an appointment booking app on short notice. By using these platforms, healthcare organizations can create functional applications in days or weeks instead of months, allowing them to respond faster to changing requirements and improve the overall patient experience.

Custom healthcare applications built on low-code and no-code platforms can address specific needs that are unique to each organization. For example, a small clinic may need an application to track patient intake forms, manage appointments, or monitor medication adherence. A larger healthcare provider may need an application to facilitate care coordination between multiple departments or to automate patient discharge workflows. These platforms provide a variety of templates and pre-built components, such as forms, patient records, and data collection tools, that can be easily customized to align with the unique workflows of healthcare providers. By enabling non-technical users to create these tailored solutions, low-code and no-code platforms reduce the dependency on IT teams, which can be overwhelmed by the high volume of software requests in large healthcare organizations.

Another important benefit of low-code and no-code platforms in healthcare is their ability to enhance collaboration between departments. Healthcare organizations typically involve a wide range of stakeholders, including clinicians, administrators, data analysts, and IT teams. The development of applications traditionally requires close coordination between these groups, which can be time-consuming and prone to miscommunication. With low-code and no-code platforms, business users from various departments can collaborate on application development directly, reducing bottlenecks and speeding up the development process. For example, a nurse might work with an administrator to create a mobile application for managing patient appointments, while an IT team ensures the integration of the application with the hospital's existing electronic health record (EHR) system. By allowing healthcare professionals to participate directly in the development process, these platforms improve the alignment between the technology and the needs of end users, ultimately leading to better outcomes for patients.

Data privacy and security are paramount in the healthcare industry, as healthcare providers are responsible for safeguarding sensitive patient information. Low-code and no-code platforms for healthcare applications often come with built-in security features, such as encrypted data storage, user authentication, and compliance with industry standards like HIPAA (Health Insurance Portability and Accountability Act). These features help ensure that applications built on these platforms adhere to strict privacy and security regulations. For example, a clinic developing a patient portal using a no-code platform can be confident that the platform will automatically handle data encryption and user access controls to protect patient information. Moreover, healthcare organizations can customize their applications to meet specific compliance requirements, such as ensuring that patient data is stored securely and that only authorized personnel can access it. By leveraging the security features provided by these platforms, healthcare organizations can build applications that protect patient privacy without requiring specialized security expertise.

The integration of various healthcare systems is a constant challenge in the industry, as hospitals, clinics, and healthcare providers rely on a variety of software applications to manage different aspects of patient care, such as EHR systems, billing software, and scheduling tools. Low-code and no-code platforms offer powerful integration capabilities that allow healthcare organizations to connect these disparate systems, enabling seamless data flow between applications. These platforms often come with pre-built connectors for popular healthcare systems, such as EHRs, patient management systems, and financial software, which makes it easier to synchronize data across different platforms. For example, a healthcare provider could use a low-code platform to create an application that automatically updates patient records in the EHR system whenever a new appointment is booked or a prescription is filled. This integration helps streamline workflows, reduce data entry errors, and ensure that all healthcare professionals have access to the most up-to-date patient information.

Additionally, low-code and no-code platforms can be used to automate key administrative tasks within healthcare organizations, improving operational efficiency and reducing manual workloads. Tasks such as scheduling, patient intake, billing, and claims processing often involve repetitive steps that can be time-consuming and error-prone. By automating these tasks through custom applications built on low-code and no-code platforms, healthcare organizations can free up valuable time for their staff to focus on patient care. For example, an automated system for processing insurance claims can be created to ensure that all necessary information is collected, verified, and submitted to insurance providers, reducing the likelihood of delays or rejections. Similarly, healthcare providers can automate appointment reminders, patient follow-up surveys, and other routine communications, ensuring a smoother experience for both patients and staff.

While low-code and no-code platforms are powerful tools for creating healthcare applications, they also allow for ongoing improvements and updates to be made in real-time. Healthcare organizations are constantly adapting to new regulations, clinical guidelines, and patient needs, and the ability to make changes quickly is crucial. With traditional software development, making updates or changes to an application could require months of coding and testing. However, with low-code and no-code platforms, healthcare providers can make changes to their applications with minimal disruption, ensuring that their software remains relevant and effective in meeting the needs of both patients and staff. This flexibility allows organizations to keep pace with the ever-changing healthcare landscape, ensuring that their technology continues to support their mission to provide high-quality care.

In addition to these benefits, low-code and no-code platforms can help improve the patient experience by enabling the development of patient-facing applications that are easy to use and accessible. From appointment scheduling and telemedicine to patient education and support, these platforms allow healthcare providers to build applications that enhance patient engagement and improve health outcomes. As the healthcare industry continues to embrace digital transformation, low-code and no-code platforms will play an increasingly important role in empowering healthcare organizations to innovate, improve operational efficiency, and deliver better patient care.

As low-code and no-code platforms continue to evolve, they will provide even more robust tools for healthcare organizations to meet their specific needs, ultimately contributing to better healthcare outcomes and a more efficient healthcare system.

Challenges in Low-Code/No-Code Application Development

Low-code and no-code platforms have gained widespread popularity in recent years, revolutionizing the way applications are built by allowing non-technical users to develop custom solutions without the need for extensive coding knowledge. These platforms have made it possible for business professionals, from marketing teams to HR departments, to create applications that address their specific needs, all while reducing the dependence on IT departments. Despite the many advantages that low-code and no-code development offer, such as faster development times and reduced costs, there are several challenges that organizations face when building applications using these platforms. Understanding these challenges is essential for businesses looking to maximize the benefits of low-code and no-code solutions while mitigating the risks associated with their use.

One of the primary challenges in low-code/no-code development is the limitation of customization and flexibility. While these platforms provide pre-built templates, components, and workflows that simplify the development process, they may not always be able to accommodate highly specific or complex requirements. For example, a business might need a feature that is not available in the platform's predefined templates or an integration that requires custom logic. In such cases, users may find themselves restricted by the capabilities of the platform. While some low-code/no-code platforms allow for limited custom code to be added, this hybrid approach can introduce complications, as users must balance the simplicity of the no-code approach with the complexity of custom code. This lack of complete flexibility can make it difficult to implement highly specialized features or meet unique business needs without running into technical limitations.

Another challenge associated with low-code/no-code development is the issue of scalability. Many low-code and no-code platforms are designed to help businesses build applications quickly for smaller-scale use cases. However, as the application grows in complexity or the user base expands, performance and scalability can become concerns. Low-code/no-code platforms may not always provide the same level of optimization or fine-tuning that custom-built applications offer, potentially leading to slow performance, security vulnerabilities, or difficulty managing increased traffic. For instance, an application that works well for a small team or department might struggle to handle the demands of a larger, organization-wide deployment. Businesses that require highly scalable applications may face challenges as their needs evolve, and they may need to invest in custom development or migrate to more robust platforms as the application grows.

Security is another critical challenge in low-code/no-code development. These platforms often involve creating applications with pre-built components that interact with sensitive data, such as customer information, financial records, or personal health data. While many platforms offer built-in security features, such as encryption, user authentication, and role-based access control, there may be gaps in how these features are configured or how they work across different components of the application. Additionally, the complexity of integrating third-party services or APIs with low-code/no-code applications can introduce security risks, particularly when dealing with external systems or legacy software. Organizations must be vigilant in ensuring that the security measures provided by the platform are correctly implemented and that they meet the necessary compliance standards for their industry, such as GDPR, HIPAA, or PCI-DSS. Failing to do so can lead to data breaches or violations of regulations, which can result in severe reputational damage and legal consequences.

One of the ongoing concerns in low-code/no-code development is the potential for shadow IT. Shadow IT refers to the use of unauthorized applications or software that are created or deployed by business users without the knowledge or approval of the IT department. While low-code and no-code platforms make it easier for business users to create applications without needing IT intervention, this can lead to a lack of oversight and control over the applications being developed. Shadow IT can create security risks, data silos, and compliance issues, especially when applications are not integrated into the organization's official IT infrastructure. IT departments may struggle to maintain visibility over the applications being created and ensure that they are secure, properly maintained, and compliant with company policies. To mitigate this risk, organizations need to establish clear governance and monitoring frameworks for low-code/no-code development, ensuring that business users are aligned with IT's security and compliance requirements.

Another challenge that businesses face when adopting low-code/no-code platforms is the potential for a lack of skilled users. While these platforms are designed to be accessible to non-technical users, there is still a learning curve, particularly for individuals who are not familiar with application design principles or the platform's specific tools. Even though the platforms provide drag-and-drop interfaces, users still need to understand how to organize data, set up workflows, and manage integrations effectively. The complexity of building an effective and user-friendly application can be overwhelming for some users, leading to a situation where the application may be underdeveloped, inefficient, or difficult for others to use. Additionally, businesses may struggle to find the right balance between empowering business users to build their own applications and ensuring that there is sufficient training and support to help them navigate the platform successfully. Without proper training or a dedicated support system, users may produce suboptimal solutions that do not fully meet business needs or fail to scale properly.

Integration with existing systems is another common challenge when using low-code and no-code platforms. While many of these platforms offer pre-built connectors for popular third-party applications, businesses often have to integrate with legacy systems or specialized software that may not be supported by the platform. Building custom integrations with these systems can require technical expertise that low-code/no-code platforms are not always equipped to provide. In such cases, businesses may find themselves struggling to connect the new applications with their existing systems, leading to data silos, inefficiencies, and a fragmented IT environment. Although some low-code/no-code platforms allow for limited custom coding to address integration issues, this approach can complicate the development process and reduce the benefits of using a no-code platform in the first place.

Performance optimization is another issue that businesses may encounter when using low-code/no-code platforms. While these platforms simplify the application development process, they may not always generate the most efficient code. Over time, as the application grows in complexity or the volume of data increases, performance can degrade. Businesses may experience slow load times, lagging user interfaces, or poor scalability as a result of the platform's limitations in generating optimized code. These performance issues can negatively impact user satisfaction and undermine the value of the application. Organizations that require high-performance applications or need to handle large volumes of data may find themselves limited by the capabilities of low-code/no-code platforms, and they may need to resort to custom development to meet their performance needs.

Finally, maintaining and updating low-code/no-code applications can be challenging over time. While these platforms enable rapid development, they also abstract much of the underlying code, which can make troubleshooting and debugging difficult. If an issue arises with the application, it may not always be clear where the problem lies, especially when the application has been built using multiple third-party components or integrations. Furthermore, as the platform evolves and new versions or features are introduced, businesses may find that their applications become incompatible or require extensive updates to maintain functionality. Organizations must ensure that they have a clear strategy for managing the long-term maintenance of low-code/no-code applications, including regular testing, updating, and monitoring for potential issues.

In summary, while low-code and no-code platforms provide many benefits, including faster development cycles, cost savings, and increased accessibility, businesses must navigate several challenges to ensure the success of their applications. These challenges include limitations in customization and flexibility, scalability concerns, security risks, the potential for shadow IT, the need for skilled users, integration difficulties, performance optimization, and long-term maintenance. By understanding these challenges and taking proactive steps to address them, businesses can harness the full potential of low-code/no-code platforms to create efficient, scalable, and secure applications that meet their needs.

Comparing Low-Code/No-Code Platforms: A Side-by-Side Overview

Low-code and no-code platforms have become pivotal in the modern development landscape, empowering organizations to rapidly build applications without the need for deep coding knowledge. As these platforms grow in popularity, businesses often find themselves choosing between the various solutions available in the market. These platforms promise to accelerate the application development process, reduce costs, and democratize access to development tools, enabling non-technical users to contribute to the creation of digital solutions. However, not all low-code/no-code platforms are created equal, and selecting the right one can be a daunting task. In this chapter, we will explore the differences and similarities between various low-code and no-code platforms, highlighting their core features, use cases, and limitations, to provide a clearer understanding of which platform is best suited for particular business needs.

When comparing low-code and no-code platforms, one of the first points of consideration is the level of customization and flexibility offered. Low-code platforms are designed to provide more customization options compared to no-code platforms. They generally offer a visual interface with drag-and-drop capabilities, similar to no-code platforms, but they also allow users to add custom code when needed. This flexibility makes low-code platforms a better choice for organizations with more complex or specialized requirements. For example, a business may need to integrate a custom database, apply advanced business logic, or connect to a proprietary service. In these cases, a low-code platform would provide the necessary tools to extend the functionality and tailor the application to the business's specific needs. On the other hand, no-code platforms are geared toward users who need to quickly create applications without writing any code. They are ideal for simpler use cases, such as creating websites, mobile apps, or small-scale internal tools, where customization and technical complexity are not a priority.

Another key distinction between low-code and no-code platforms lies in the types of users they are designed for. Low-code platforms are often targeted at developers or technical users who want to speed up the development process by minimizing the amount of manual coding required. These platforms are designed for those with at least some programming knowledge, allowing them to build more complex applications while still benefiting from visual design tools. Developers can create applications with custom workflows, integrations, and logic, all without starting from scratch. No-code platforms, on the other hand, are specifically designed for non-technical users. These platforms offer intuitive, drag-and-drop interfaces that enable business users, such as marketers, HR professionals, and department heads, to build applications without writing any code. The simplicity of no-code platforms makes them ideal for those who lack technical expertise but still need to create basic applications quickly. As a result, no-code platforms tend to be more accessible to a broader range of users, while low-code platforms may require a higher level of technical skill to fully leverage.

The types of applications each platform can support also differ. Low-code platforms are capable of handling more complex, enterprise-level applications that require robust functionality, advanced workflows, and integrations with other systems. These platforms allow users to build everything from CRM systems to data management tools and even custom workflows for enterprise resource planning (ERP). No-code platforms, by contrast, are more suited to simpler applications such as landing pages, basic mobile apps, and internal tools for small teams. While no-code platforms may offer some integration capabilities, their primary strength lies in enabling rapid application creation for straightforward tasks. Low-code platforms offer a broader range of use cases and are often the preferred choice for organizations that need applications with complex business rules, third-party integrations, or custom logic.

Integration capabilities are another important factor when comparing low-code and no-code platforms. Low-code platforms generally excel in this area, offering a wide variety of pre-built connectors to integrate with external systems, databases, and third-party services. These platforms support APIs, allowing developers to create custom integrations or modify existing ones to connect disparate systems. For example, a low-code platform may enable seamless integration with a customer relationship management (CRM) system, an accounting platform, or an inventory management solution. No-code platforms, while also supporting integrations, typically offer fewer options and may limit users to using pre-built connectors. These integrations may be sufficient for smaller applications or those that rely on a few widely-used services, but for more complex integrations, low-code platforms are often the better choice.

Scalability is another area where low-code and no-code platforms differ significantly. Low-code platforms are generally better suited for building scalable applications that can grow with the organization. These platforms are designed to handle larger user bases, more complex workflows, and higher data volumes. As organizations expand, low-code applications can be adjusted and modified to accommodate new needs, such as adding additional features or expanding user access. No-code platforms, on the other hand, are more limited in their ability to scale. While they can be used to create smaller applications for individual teams or departments, they may struggle to meet the demands of a growing enterprise. The simplicity of no-code platforms makes them ideal for smaller, short-term projects, but they may not be able to handle the complexity of large-scale deployments.

Cost is often a determining factor for businesses when choosing between low-code and no-code platforms. No-code platforms are generally more affordable, as they are designed for quick, simple development and can be used by non-technical users. The cost of these platforms is often based on a subscription model, which may be lower than the costs associated with low-code platforms. In contrast, low-code platforms tend to be more expensive due to the increased level of customization and support they provide. These platforms are typically priced based on the number of users, the level of customization, and the complexity of the application being built. For organizations with a small budget or for those looking to build simple applications, no-code platforms are an attractive option. However, for larger organizations or those with more complex needs, low-code platforms offer the flexibility and scalability necessary to meet those demands, even if they come at a higher price point.

Support and resources also vary between low-code and no-code platforms. Low-code platforms often offer more robust support for developers, including access to documentation, APIs, and technical resources to help users create more sophisticated applications. These platforms may also provide dedicated customer support and enterprise-grade services to assist with the implementation of large-scale solutions. No-code platforms, while still offering support, typically provide fewer resources for developers and are more focused on providing easy-to-understand guides, templates, and user-friendly interfaces for non-technical users. While no-code platforms are great for businesses with limited technical resources, organizations that require deeper technical support may find low-code platforms to be a better fit.

As low-code and no-code platforms continue to evolve, many of the distinctions between them are becoming less pronounced. Some platforms now offer a hybrid approach, combining the ease of use of no-code tools with the customization and integration capabilities of low-code platforms. These hybrid solutions aim to provide the best of both worlds, allowing non-technical users to create basic applications while giving developers the ability to build more complex solutions when necessary. This trend towards convergence is indicative of the growing demand for flexible, user-friendly platforms that can cater to a wide range of business needs.

In summary, the choice between low-code and no-code platforms depends on the complexity of the application being developed, the technical expertise of the users, the scale of the project, and the budget available. Low-code platforms are ideal for more complex, scalable solutions that require deep customization and integration with other systems, while no-code platforms are better suited for simpler, smaller-scale applications. Understanding the strengths and limitations of each platform is crucial for businesses looking to leverage low-code and no-code tools effectively to meet their unique needs. By carefully evaluating these factors, businesses can select the platform that best supports their objectives and accelerates their development efforts.

How Low-Code/No-Code Platforms Enable Citizen Developers

The rise of low-code and no-code platforms has fundamentally changed the landscape of software development, enabling non-technical users to create applications with little to no coding knowledge. These platforms have empowered a new class of creators, known as citizen developers, who can now build custom solutions to meet their specific business needs. Citizen developers are typically business users with domain expertise in areas such as sales, marketing, finance, or operations, but who lack formal training in software development. By providing user-friendly, visual interfaces and pre-built components, low-code and no-code platforms allow these individuals to participate in application development and innovation, bypassing traditional IT departments and accelerating the time-to-market for custom solutions.

One of the core features of low-code and no-code platforms is the simplicity of their interfaces, which allow users to build applications without needing to write complex code. These platforms use drag-and-drop tools, visual workflows, and pre-configured templates to help users design, customize, and deploy applications. Citizen developers can leverage these features to create everything from simple internal tools and mobile apps to more complex enterprise applications, all tailored to their specific workflows. For example, a marketing professional can use a no-code platform to create a customer relationship management (CRM) system or an automated email marketing campaign tool, without having to rely on the IT department or learn to code. This democratization of application development empowers business users to take control of their own digital solutions and ensures that the tools they create are closely aligned with their business needs.

The growth of citizen development is closely tied to the increasing demand for personalized, agile, and quickly deployable software solutions. Traditional software development is often slow and resource-intensive, with long lead times and high costs associated with building custom applications. In many cases, IT departments are overwhelmed by the sheer volume of software requests from various departments within the organization, and this can lead to delays in addressing business needs. Low-code and no-code platforms address this issue by allowing business users to develop their own solutions, bypassing the bottleneck created by traditional development processes. This enables organizations to respond more quickly to changing market conditions, customer demands, and internal requirements.

Another major benefit of empowering citizen developers is the ability to foster greater innovation within an organization. Because citizen developers are intimately familiar with the day-to-day operations and challenges of their respective departments, they are in a unique position to identify opportunities for process improvements and create tools that address specific pain points. For example, an HR manager might use a low-code platform to build a custom employee onboarding application that streamlines the hiring process, reduces manual paperwork, and improves the new employee experience. By allowing these users to develop solutions tailored to their domain expertise, businesses can unlock a wealth of innovative ideas that may not have been captured by traditional IT development teams.

Low-code and no-code platforms also promote collaboration between business units and IT departments. While citizen developers are creating their own applications, they often collaborate with IT teams to ensure that their solutions align with the organization's overall infrastructure, security policies, and data governance standards. IT departments can act as advisors, providing oversight and guidance on best practices, security protocols, and system integrations, while still allowing business users to drive the development process. This collaboration enables businesses to create applications that are both business-driven and technically sound, without sacrificing agility or innovation. Additionally, IT teams can focus on more complex, enterprise-wide projects while empowering citizen developers to address departmental-specific needs.

Despite the many benefits, there are also challenges associated with enabling citizen developers. One of the most significant concerns is the potential for inconsistent or suboptimal application development. While low-code and no-code platforms make it easy for non-technical users to build applications, they may lack the deep technical expertise needed to design scalable, efficient, and secure solutions. Citizen developers may not be aware of industry best practices, which can lead to issues with performance, security, or data integration. To mitigate this risk, businesses must provide citizen developers with proper training, support, and governance frameworks. IT departments can offer guidance on topics such as data security, system integration, and application maintenance, helping citizen developers create solutions that meet both business and technical standards.

Security and compliance are also critical considerations when enabling citizen development. As citizen developers create applications that handle sensitive data or interact with other business systems, it is essential to ensure that these applications adhere to the organization's security policies and regulatory requirements. Low-code and no-code platforms often include built-in security features such as role-based access controls, data encryption, and compliance with industry standards like GDPR and HIPAA. However, organizations must also ensure that citizen developers understand the importance of securing sensitive data and adhering to compliance regulations. By providing training on data protection and ensuring that security features are properly configured, businesses can minimize the risks associated with citizen development.

Another challenge is the long-term maintenance and scalability of applications built by citizen developers. While these applications may meet immediate business needs, they may not always be designed with scalability or future growth in mind. As business requirements evolve, citizen-developed applications may need to be updated or integrated with other systems. IT departments play a crucial role in ensuring that these applications are properly maintained, updated, and scaled to meet the changing needs of the organization. By establishing clear processes for application lifecycle management, businesses can ensure that citizen-developed applications remain effective and secure over time.

The rise of citizen developers has also led to the need for better governance and oversight of low-code/no-code platforms. Organizations must establish guidelines for who can create applications, what types of applications are permissible, and how these applications are maintained and updated. Without proper governance, there is a risk of creating redundant or incompatible applications that could lead to data silos or inefficiencies within the organization. A well-defined governance framework can help ensure that citizen development aligns with the organization's overall digital strategy, minimizes risks, and maximizes the value of low-code/no-code platforms. This framework should include approval processes for new applications, documentation standards, and periodic reviews of applications to ensure they continue to meet business and technical requirements.

Despite these challenges, the benefits of empowering citizen developers far outweigh the potential drawbacks. By providing business users with the tools to create their own applications, low-code and no-code platforms not only reduce the burden on IT teams but also foster a culture of innovation, collaboration, and agility within organizations. Citizen developers can quickly build solutions that address specific business needs, improve processes, and enhance the overall customer experience. As these platforms continue to evolve, the role of citizen developers will only become more important, helping businesses stay competitive in an increasingly digital world. By providing the right training, governance, and support, organizations can unlock the full potential of low-code/no-code platforms and enable their employees to become active contributors to the digital transformation journey.

Automation with Low-Code/No-Code for Business Efficiency

In today's fast-paced business environment, efficiency is crucial for organizations looking to stay competitive and meet customer demands. Automation has become a cornerstone of this efficiency, helping businesses streamline their operations, reduce manual labor, and improve overall productivity. However, traditional automation often requires specialized technical expertise, which can be a barrier for many organizations. This is where low-code and no-code platforms have come into play, providing businesses with the ability to automate their processes without needing extensive coding knowledge. By allowing non-technical users to create automation workflows, these platforms have democratized automation and empowered business users to take control of their own processes, leading to significant improvements in business efficiency.

One of the primary ways that low-code and no-code platforms facilitate automation is through their visual, drag-and-drop interfaces. These platforms offer intuitive tools that enable business users to design automation workflows with minimal effort. For example, a marketing team can use a no-code platform to automatically send follow-up emails to customers after a purchase or schedule social media posts based on pre-defined triggers. Similarly, an HR department might automate the onboarding process, ensuring that all new employees receive the necessary documents, training materials, and access to internal systems without the need for manual intervention. By using these visual tools, business users can quickly map out the steps involved in a process and automate repetitive tasks, which significantly reduces the risk of errors and frees up time for more strategic activities.

The ability to integrate multiple systems is another key feature of low-code and no-code platforms that enhances business efficiency through automation. Many businesses rely on a variety of software applications to manage different aspects of their operations, such as customer relationship management (CRM), enterprise resource planning (ERP), human resources, and marketing automation. These platforms offer built-in connectors to integrate with a wide range of third-party services and databases, enabling seamless data transfer and synchronization across systems. For example, a low-code platform can be used to create an automated workflow that pulls customer data from a CRM, processes it, and sends it to a marketing platform for targeted email campaigns. The integration of different systems ensures that data flows effortlessly across the organization, eliminating the need for manual data entry and reducing the likelihood of errors.

Another benefit of automation with low-code and no-code platforms is the ability to scale operations without increasing the burden on staff. As businesses grow, so does the complexity and volume of tasks that need to be managed. Without automation, businesses would need to hire more employees to handle these increasing demands, which can be costly and time-consuming. By automating routine tasks, businesses can handle larger volumes of work without needing to expand their workforce significantly. For example, an e-commerce company might use automation to manage inventory, process orders, and handle customer inquiries. As the business scales, the same automation workflows can be adjusted or extended to accommodate the growing demands, without requiring additional human resources or a complete overhaul of the systems.

Low-code and no-code automation also empower organizations to respond more quickly to changing business needs and market conditions. Traditional automation processes often involve lengthy development cycles, requiring significant investment in time and resources to implement changes. In contrast, low-code and no-code platforms allow businesses to make changes to automation workflows in real-time, enabling them to adapt quickly to shifting priorities or emerging opportunities. For example, if a company needs to change its marketing strategy or update its product inventory, the business can use a low-code platform to quickly modify existing workflows or create new automation processes that align with the updated strategy. This level of agility ensures that businesses can remain competitive and responsive in a fast-paced environment.

Furthermore, low-code and no-code automation platforms can improve business efficiency by reducing reliance on manual interventions and minimizing human error. Many business processes, especially those that involve repetitive tasks or large volumes of data, are prone to mistakes when done manually. Automation eliminates the risk of human error by ensuring that tasks are completed consistently and accurately. For instance, an accounts payable department can use an automated workflow to process invoices, verify payment terms, and send reminders for overdue payments. By automating this process, businesses can reduce the risk of mistakes, such as missed payments or incorrect data entry, that can lead to financial discrepancies or delays. This results in a more reliable and efficient workflow, allowing employees to focus on higher-value tasks that require critical thinking and problem-solving.

The speed at which low-code and no-code platforms enable the creation and deployment of automated workflows is another factor that contributes to improved business efficiency. Traditional automation solutions often require months of planning, development, and testing before they are ready to be deployed. In contrast, low-code and no-code platforms allow businesses to implement automation much more quickly. Users can design, test, and deploy workflows in a fraction of the time it would take with traditional methods, accelerating the time-to-market for new processes and applications. This rapid deployment is especially beneficial for organizations that need to quickly adjust to new business requirements or customer demands.

Moreover, the democratization of automation through low-code and no-code platforms leads to greater innovation across the organization. In many companies, employees who are closest to the processes—such as sales representatives, customer service agents, and operations managers—are often the best positioned to identify inefficiencies and suggest improvements. Low-code and no-code platforms give these employees the tools to create and implement automation workflows that address their specific challenges. This encourages innovation at all levels of the organization, as employees are empowered to take ownership of their processes and contribute to continuous improvement. As a result, businesses can foster a culture of innovation, where employees are motivated to find new ways to enhance efficiency and effectiveness.

One of the challenges that businesses face when implementing automation is ensuring that the automated workflows are secure and compliant with industry regulations. Low-code and no-code platforms address this concern by offering built-in security features, such as data encryption, role-based access control, and audit trails, to ensure that sensitive data is protected and that automation workflows adhere to compliance standards. Additionally, these platforms typically provide tools for monitoring and auditing workflows, making it easier to track the performance of automated processes and identify any potential issues or areas for improvement. This oversight is essential for ensuring that automated workflows are running as intended and that they remain secure and compliant over time.

While low-code and no-code platforms offer a wide range of benefits, there are some limitations to consider when using them for automation. These platforms are best suited for automating less complex processes, and while they can handle a wide variety of tasks, they may not be the best fit for highly specialized or intricate automation needs. Businesses that require more advanced automation capabilities or that need to integrate with complex systems may need to supplement low-code/no-code platforms with custom-built solutions or more advanced automation tools. However, for most businesses, these platforms offer a powerful way to automate routine tasks, increase operational efficiency, and improve productivity without the need for specialized technical skills.

In conclusion, low-code and no-code platforms are transforming the way businesses approach automation, enabling organizations to streamline processes, reduce costs, and improve overall efficiency. These platforms allow business users to design and deploy automation workflows quickly, without relying on IT teams, and they provide a flexible and scalable solution for managing increasingly complex tasks. By empowering employees to create and implement automation solutions, businesses can improve their agility, enhance customer experiences, and foster a culture of innovation, all while achieving significant gains in productivity and operational efficiency.

Exploring the Role of APIs in Low-Code/No-Code Development

The rapid growth of low-code and no-code platforms has revolutionized the way applications are developed, enabling users with limited or no coding expertise to create functional solutions for various business needs. One of the critical components that empower these platforms is the use of application programming interfaces (APIs). APIs serve as bridges between different software systems, allowing them to communicate with each other and share data seamlessly. In the context of low-code and no-code development, APIs play a vital role in extending the capabilities of the platform, enabling non-technical users to build more complex and integrated applications. The integration of APIs into low-code and no-code platforms significantly enhances their power, making them not just tools for simple app creation but gateways for businesses to create robust, scalable solutions.

APIs provide a way for low-code and no-code platforms to interact with external systems, databases, and services. Many low-code platforms offer built-in connectors that allow users to easily integrate with third-party APIs, such as customer relationship management (CRM) tools, social media platforms, payment gateways, and cloud services. These connectors simplify the process of connecting external data sources to the application being developed, enabling users to build applications that are more dynamic and capable of interacting with a variety of systems. For example, a business user can use a no-code platform to build a custom application that pulls data from an existing CRM system, integrates it with an email marketing tool, and displays relevant customer information on a dashboard, all without writing a single line of code. This ability to integrate data and functionality from external systems is what makes low-code and no-code platforms so powerful in addressing a wide range of business needs.

Beyond integration, APIs enable automation within low-code and no-code applications. By linking various systems and processes, APIs allow users to automate workflows and tasks that would otherwise require manual intervention. For example, a business user can create a low-code application that automatically updates inventory levels in a warehouse management system when an order is placed through an e-commerce platform. The use of APIs in this context ensures that the application is connected to the right systems and can automatically trigger actions based on specific events or conditions. This reduces the need for manual data entry, minimizes human error, and increases the overall efficiency of business processes. Automation through APIs also enables businesses to respond more quickly to changes in the market or customer needs, as workflows can be adjusted in real-time without requiring significant changes to the underlying infrastructure.

APIs also play a critical role in extending the functionality of low-code and no-code applications. While these platforms offer a wide range of pre-built components and templates, there are times when a business user may need more advanced features or specific functionality that is not available out-of-the-box. In such cases, APIs allow users to extend their applications by integrating custom code or third-party services. For instance, a user might want to incorporate advanced data analytics or machine learning models into their application. By connecting to APIs that provide these services, a non-technical user can enhance the application's capabilities without needing to understand the complexities of the underlying technology. This flexibility is one of the key reasons why APIs are so valuable in the low-code and no-code ecosystem, as they enable users to create highly customized applications that meet specific business needs.

Furthermore, APIs contribute to the scalability of low-code and no-code applications. As businesses grow and their needs become more complex, the applications they use must be able to scale accordingly. Low-code and no-code platforms, in conjunction with APIs, allow applications to integrate with more robust systems and handle larger volumes of data. For example, a small business might start by using a no-code platform to build a simple customer management app, but as the business grows, it may need to integrate the app with more powerful backend systems or cloud services to handle increased data processing and storage. APIs make this scalability possible by providing a standardized way to connect to these systems. As a result, businesses can continue to build on the applications they've developed with low-code or no-code platforms, adding new features and integrations as needed, without having to completely rebuild their solutions from scratch.

The role of APIs in low-code and no-code development also extends to improving user experience and accessibility. APIs enable the creation of more interactive and dynamic applications by allowing real-time data updates and interactions between systems. For example, an application that provides real-time stock market data can use APIs to pull the latest data from financial markets and update the user interface instantly, providing users with the most current information. This enhances the overall user experience, making the application more engaging and relevant to the end user. Additionally, APIs allow low-code and no-code applications to connect to various platforms, such as mobile devices, social media, and cloud-based services, increasing accessibility and ensuring that users can interact with the application from multiple devices and environments.

One of the significant advantages of APIs in low-code and no-code development is their role in ensuring data consistency and integrity across systems. When building applications that rely on multiple data sources, it is essential to ensure that the data is synchronized and accurate. APIs facilitate this by allowing low-code and no-code applications to automatically pull and update data from various systems, ensuring that all components of the application are using the most up-to-date information. For example, an order management system built on a low-code platform can use APIs to synchronize inventory levels, customer information, and financial records in real-time, reducing the risk of discrepancies or outdated data. This synchronization is crucial for maintaining business operations and delivering reliable services to customers.

Despite their many advantages, using APIs in low-code and no-code development can present challenges. One of the most common challenges is ensuring proper API management. As more systems are integrated through APIs, the complexity of managing these connections increases. It is essential for businesses to ensure that the APIs are properly authenticated, monitored, and maintained. Poorly managed APIs can lead to security vulnerabilities, data breaches, or integration failures. Furthermore, businesses must also account for the potential impact of changes to third-party APIs. If an external service updates its API or changes its functionality, it may disrupt the integrations in low-code and no-code applications, requiring the business to make adjustments to their workflows. To mitigate these risks, businesses must implement proper API management practices, such as regular testing, version control, and monitoring.

APIs also create dependencies on external services, which can present challenges if those services experience downtime or outages. For example, if a third-party payment gateway API becomes unavailable, an application relying on that service for transactions may fail. Therefore, businesses need to carefully consider the reliability and availability of the APIs they integrate into their low-code and no-code applications. Ensuring that they use reputable, well-documented, and supported APIs can help minimize these risks.

In summary, APIs play an essential role in the functionality, scalability, and customization of low-code and no-code applications. They enable seamless integration with external systems, automate workflows, extend functionality, and ensure real-time data updates, all of which contribute to the overall effectiveness of the applications. Despite the challenges associated with managing and maintaining API connections, the benefits they offer in terms of enhancing business processes and creating more dynamic, customized applications make them an indispensable tool for low-code and no-code development. As the demand for more complex and integrated applications grows, the importance of APIs in the low-code/no-code ecosystem will continue to rise, driving innovation and empowering businesses to create solutions that meet their unique needs.

Navigating the Learning Curve in Low-Code/No-Code Platforms

The rise of low-code and no-code platforms has empowered a broad range of users—from business analysts and marketers to HR professionals and operations managers—to create applications that solve specific problems without the need for deep programming expertise. These platforms promise to democratize application development, enabling users to design, build, and deploy software solutions with little to no coding experience. However, despite their promise of simplicity and accessibility, these platforms come with their own set of challenges, particularly when it comes to the learning curve that users must navigate to use them effectively. Understanding how to approach this learning curve is essential for businesses looking to maximize the potential of low-code and no-code platforms, ensuring that non-technical users can leverage these tools without getting overwhelmed.

At first glance, low-code and no-code platforms appear to be user-friendly, offering intuitive drag-and-drop interfaces and visual development tools. However, the simplicity of these interfaces can be deceiving, as they still require users to understand how to structure applications, design workflows, and manage data. Many platforms offer pre-built templates and components that allow users to quickly put together an application, but users still need to know how to customize these elements to meet their specific needs. For example, a marketing professional may be able to create a simple landing page using pre-designed templates but may struggle when trying to integrate the landing page with an existing customer relationship management (CRM) system. While the platform may not require coding, it still necessitates a level of understanding about how different elements of the application interact with one another, as well as an awareness of best practices in design and functionality.

One of the main challenges that users face when learning to use low-code and no-code platforms is understanding the underlying logic and structure of application development. Even though these platforms abstract away much of the technical complexity, they still rely on a set of foundational principles, such as how data is organized, how user interactions are captured, and how workflows are automated. Users must understand these principles to build functional and efficient applications. For instance, when building an application that collects customer data, a user needs to comprehend how data flows between forms, how it is stored, and how it is processed within the application. Without a solid understanding of these underlying concepts, even a visually simple application can become disorganized, inefficient, or difficult to scale. This gap in knowledge can be a significant part of the learning curve, as users must not only familiarize themselves with the platform's specific tools but also grasp basic application design concepts.

Another challenge in learning low-code and no-code platforms is the platform's documentation and resources. While many platforms provide comprehensive tutorials, help guides, and community support, the learning experience can still feel overwhelming for new users. Low-code and no-code platforms often come with a wide range of features and capabilities, and navigating these options can be a daunting task, especially when trying to build something more complex than a basic application. While documentation is often available, it is not always written in a way that is accessible to non-technical users. For example, a business user who has never worked with application development may find technical jargon confusing, even if the underlying concepts are relatively simple. In these situations, businesses may need to invest additional resources into training or support services to ensure that users can effectively learn how to use the platform. Without proper guidance, users might become frustrated, potentially leading to inefficient application development or abandonment of the platform altogether.

The learning curve is also influenced by the level of customization that the user needs to implement. While no-code platforms are generally more restrictive in terms of customization, low-code platforms provide greater flexibility, which can increase the complexity of the development process. For users who need to create custom logic, integrate external systems, or build advanced workflows, low-code platforms require a deeper understanding of the platform's capabilities. While they allow for code to be inserted in specific areas of the application, users still need to understand where and how to add this code effectively. A user with limited technical experience may find it difficult to implement advanced functionality, such as building a complex approval workflow or creating custom APIs, without a basic understanding of programming concepts. This can make low-code platforms more challenging for users who do not have a technical background, even though they offer more power and customization than no-code alternatives.

Furthermore, as low-code and no-code platforms become more advanced, their functionalities and features also increase in complexity. For example, some platforms offer integration with external databases, API connections, and advanced automation features. While these capabilities can be extremely useful, they add an additional layer of complexity for users. A user who is comfortable with the basic features of the platform may struggle when trying to connect their application to third-party services or build more sophisticated automation. Understanding how to integrate these services, manage authentication, and troubleshoot potential issues requires a higher level of technical know-how, which may not be immediately intuitive for non-technical users.

Despite these challenges, the learning curve associated with low-code and no-code platforms can be navigated successfully with the right approach. One of the most effective strategies is to begin with simpler projects and gradually increase the complexity as the user becomes more comfortable with the platform. Many users make the mistake of diving into complex applications right away, only to become overwhelmed by the platform's many features. By starting small, users can gain confidence in their abilities, learning how to create simple applications before moving on to more advanced functionality. This step-by-step approach allows users to develop a solid understanding of the platform's tools and concepts, ensuring that they can build on their knowledge and avoid feeling frustrated by the process.

In addition, taking advantage of the platform's training resources is crucial for overcoming the learning curve. Many low-code and no-code platforms offer tutorials, videos, and community forums where users can learn from others and share best practices. These resources can provide valuable insights into how the platform works, as well as offer tips and tricks for building better applications. Engaging with the platform's community can also be a great way for users to get help with specific issues they may encounter during the development process. For businesses, investing in formal training for employees can help accelerate the learning process and ensure that employees have the skills they need to use the platform effectively.

Mentorship and support from more experienced users or IT departments can also help ease the transition to using low-code and no-code platforms. While these platforms are designed to be accessible to non-technical users, having a technical expert available to provide guidance can make the learning process smoother and more efficient. IT departments can offer valuable insights into how to structure applications, integrate systems, and ensure security, which can be especially important for businesses that are looking to build more complex or enterprise-level applications.

Ultimately, while the learning curve for low-code and no-code platforms may seem steep at first, it can be overcome with patience, practice, and the right resources. As users become more familiar with the tools and the underlying principles of application development, they will gain the confidence and expertise needed to build powerful applications that meet the specific needs of their organization. With the right approach, the potential of low-code and no-code platforms can be fully realized, enabling businesses to create innovative solutions and streamline their operations. The key is to take it one step at a time, gradually building skills and knowledge while leveraging the support available within the platform's community and resources.

Designing and Deploying Workflow Automation

In the ever-evolving business landscape, efficiency is crucial, and workflow automation has become a key driver in achieving it. By automating repetitive tasks and streamlining complex processes, businesses can reduce errors, improve productivity, and allocate resources more effectively. Designing and deploying workflow automation involves understanding the tasks that can be automated, creating seamless workflows, and ensuring that they integrate well with existing systems. The power of workflow automation lies in its ability to replace manual work with automated, error-free processes, which leads to more streamlined operations and enhanced business outcomes. While traditionally, workflow automation required extensive technical expertise and custom coding, low-code and no-code platforms have democratized the process, allowing non-technical users to design and deploy these systems with ease.

The first step in designing workflow automation is identifying the processes that would benefit the most from automation. Not every task or workflow is suitable for automation, so understanding which areas can be optimized is critical. Businesses should start by mapping out their existing workflows to pinpoint bottlenecks, repetitive tasks, and areas prone to human error. For example, manual data entry, document approvals, and customer service inquiries are common candidates for automation. A common approach is to automate tasks that involve the transfer of data between systems, such as automatically updating a CRM with new customer information, or sending notifications when an action is required. Once these workflows are identified, it becomes easier to design automation that improves efficiency and reduces the need for manual intervention.

After identifying the tasks to automate, businesses must design the workflow itself. This is where low-code and no-code platforms come into play, offering intuitive drag-and-drop interfaces that allow users to design their workflows visually. These platforms offer a variety of pre-built components such as forms, actions, and triggers that can be easily assembled to create a flow that mimics the steps of the manual process. For instance, a user might create an automated workflow that triggers when a new order is placed, processes payment, updates inventory, and sends an order confirmation to the customer. These workflows can involve multiple steps and integrate with various systems without the need for custom coding, making the process far more accessible to non-technical users.

The design phase also involves setting the rules and conditions that determine when and how the workflow is executed. For example, if a task is dependent on the completion of a previous task, such as the approval of a purchase request, the automation can be designed to wait until the approval is granted before proceeding. Defining these conditional steps ensures that the workflow follows a logical path and does not proceed until the required conditions are met. By incorporating these rules, businesses can create highly customized workflows that reflect their unique needs and ensure that operations run smoothly.

In addition to defining steps and rules, the integration of data sources is a key consideration when designing workflow automation. Most businesses rely on multiple systems to manage different aspects of their operations, such as CRM platforms, marketing tools, accounting systems, and email services. A successful workflow must seamlessly integrate with these systems to ensure data flows consistently and accurately between them. Many low-code and no-code platforms offer pre-built integrations with popular third-party applications, allowing users to quickly connect their workflows to external systems. For example, integrating an automated order processing workflow with an e-commerce platform and an inventory management system ensures that once an order is placed, inventory is updated in real-time, and the customer receives immediate confirmation of their purchase.

Once the workflow has been designed and integrated with necessary systems, the next step is deploying the automation. Deployment involves testing the workflow to ensure that it functions as expected and is fully integrated with the various systems it relies on. Many low-code and no-code platforms provide testing environments where users can simulate workflows before deploying them live. These testing tools help identify any issues, such as missing data or incorrect logic, and allow businesses to address them before the workflow goes into production. Once the workflow passes testing, it can be deployed, which means it will start executing automatically based on the triggers and conditions defined during the design phase. Deployment also involves ensuring that the automation is accessible to the appropriate users and that they have the necessary permissions to interact with it. This is particularly important when workflows involve sensitive data or require approval from certain individuals before proceeding.

Monitoring and maintaining the workflow is another important part of deployment. While low-code and no-code platforms simplify the process of building and deploying workflows, they still require oversight to ensure that they continue to operate smoothly. Once the automation is live, businesses must monitor its performance to identify any potential issues, such as system downtimes or bottlenecks that slow the process. Most platforms provide tools for tracking the performance of workflows, offering insights into how long each task takes to complete, how many tasks are in progress, and whether there are any errors in the process. This data allows businesses to make adjustments and optimizations as needed, ensuring that workflows continue to run efficiently and deliver the desired outcomes.

Additionally, ongoing maintenance and updates are essential to keep the workflow relevant as business needs change. Workflow automation is not a one-time setup but an ongoing process that requires periodic review and refinement. Over time, businesses may need to adjust workflows to account for changes in regulations, customer preferences, or internal processes. For instance, a business may need to add new steps to a workflow to account for updated compliance requirements or add additional actions as new systems are integrated into the process. Low-code and no-code platforms make it easy to make these changes, as users can modify the workflow with just a few clicks, without needing to redevelop the entire system.

The role of user feedback cannot be overlooked in the deployment of workflow automation. Even though workflows are designed to be automated, they often involve human intervention at some point, whether it's approving a task or entering specific data. Collecting feedback from the users interacting with the automation helps ensure that it is functioning as intended and meeting business objectives. Feedback can also highlight areas for improvement or adjustment, making it an essential part of the process. Businesses should create a feedback loop to assess the effectiveness of the workflow, gather insights, and implement necessary changes to improve the automation's performance.

Ultimately, workflow automation can greatly enhance business efficiency by streamlining tasks, reducing manual labor, and improving accuracy. Low-code and no-code platforms have made it easier than ever to design and deploy these automation systems, allowing business users to take control of their workflows without relying on IT departments or developers. By following a structured approach to design, deployment, and ongoing monitoring, businesses can ensure that their automated workflows deliver long-term value, helping them operate more efficiently and stay competitive in an increasingly fast-paced marketplace. These platforms enable organizations to create robust solutions that automate a wide range of business processes, from simple tasks to complex, multi-step workflows, all while making the process accessible to users of all technical skill levels.

Building Enterprise Solutions with Low-Code/No-Code

In recent years, low-code and no-code platforms have emerged as powerful tools for businesses seeking to develop enterprise-level solutions without the need for extensive technical expertise. Traditionally, enterprise solutions required dedicated IT teams, large budgets, and long development cycles to meet the complex needs of large organizations. These solutions often involved custom coding, which could be time-consuming and costly. Low-code and no-code platforms have revolutionized this approach by providing intuitive, visual interfaces that allow both technical and non-technical users to create applications quickly and efficiently. As businesses face increasing pressure to innovate and respond rapidly to market changes, these platforms are becoming essential tools in the development of enterprise solutions.

Building enterprise solutions using low-code and no-code platforms begins with understanding the complexity of enterprise requirements. Enterprise solutions often involve large-scale operations, including integrations with multiple systems, data management, workflow automation, and user access controls. While these tasks may seem daunting, low-code and no-code platforms are designed to simplify these processes. These platforms provide a range of pre-built templates, components, and integrations that can help businesses create applications that meet the unique demands of enterprise environments. For example, a business could use a low-code platform to build a customer relationship management (CRM) system that integrates with an existing enterprise resource planning (ERP) system, a marketing automation tool, and a customer service platform. This integration ensures that all the data is synchronized, improving operational efficiency and enhancing the user experience.

One of the primary advantages of using low-code and no-code platforms for building enterprise solutions is the speed with which applications can be developed and deployed. Traditionally, the development of enterprise applications could take months or even years, requiring complex coding and rigorous testing phases. With low-code and no-code platforms, businesses can develop applications in a fraction of that time. These platforms allow users to visually design and configure applications using drag-and-drop features, enabling non-technical users to contribute to the development process. This accelerates the time-to-market for new solutions, allowing businesses to respond quickly to changing market conditions and customer demands. Additionally, the ease of customization offered by these platforms ensures that applications can be tailored to the specific needs of the business, without sacrificing functionality.

Despite the ease of use, building enterprise solutions with low-code and no-code platforms does require a deep understanding of the business's needs. These platforms offer the flexibility to create applications that align with organizational goals, but it is up to the business leaders and users to define what those needs are and how the application should function. This requires careful planning and collaboration across departments to ensure that the application meets the diverse needs of all stakeholders. For example, an application designed to streamline HR processes might need to accommodate various user roles, from HR managers to employees, while ensuring that data privacy and compliance requirements are met. The ability to map out workflows, user permissions, and data access in a visual manner is a powerful feature of low-code and no-code platforms, but it requires clear communication and collaboration within the organization to get it right.

One of the challenges in building enterprise solutions with low-code and no-code platforms is the need to ensure scalability. While these platforms are incredibly efficient for developing small to medium-sized applications, they must also be able to scale as the organization grows. Enterprise solutions need to handle large amounts of data, support thousands of users, and integrate with various internal and external systems. Low-code and no-code platforms are increasingly capable of handling these demands, but businesses must ensure that the platform they choose can meet their scalability needs. Many modern low-code platforms are built on cloud infrastructure, allowing for seamless scaling, but it is important to consider factors such as load balancing, data storage, and performance optimization when designing an enterprise solution.

Security and compliance are other crucial considerations when building enterprise solutions. Enterprises are often subject to strict regulatory requirements, such as the General Data Protection Regulation (GDPR) or the Health Insurance Portability and Accountability Act (HIPAA), which govern how customer data should be handled, stored, and protected. Low-code and no-code platforms provide a variety of security features, such as role-based access control, data encryption, and audit logs, which help businesses ensure that their applications comply with industry regulations. However, these platforms can only provide security at the application level, and businesses must also implement broader security measures at the organizational level. This includes ensuring that APIs are secure, data is backed up, and proper access controls are in place to prevent unauthorized users from accessing sensitive information. While low-code and no-code platforms simplify many aspects of security, businesses must still take an active role in ensuring that their applications are secure and compliant.

Another benefit of using low-code and no-code platforms for building enterprise solutions is the ease of integration with existing systems. Enterprises typically rely on a wide range of software tools and databases to manage their operations, including accounting software, HR systems, marketing platforms, and customer service applications. Low-code and no-code platforms offer pre-built connectors and integration options that make it easy to connect new applications to these existing systems. This reduces the complexity of integrating disparate tools and ensures that data flows seamlessly across platforms. For example, a low-code platform might allow a company to create a custom dashboard that pulls data from its ERP system, CRM platform, and marketing tools, providing a unified view of key business metrics. These integrations help to break down silos within the organization and improve data accessibility and decision-making.

Customization is another key factor in building enterprise solutions with low-code and no-code platforms. While these platforms offer pre-built components and templates, they also allow businesses to customize the applications to meet their specific needs. Customization can range from simple changes, such as adjusting the user interface or adding custom branding, to more complex modifications, such as integrating new features or creating custom business logic. Low-code platforms provide a higher degree of flexibility for customization, as they allow users to write custom code when needed. This ensures that businesses can create applications that not only fit their current needs but can also be easily updated and extended as their requirements evolve over time.

Once the enterprise solution has been developed, deploying the application is the next critical step. Low-code and no-code platforms typically offer cloud-based deployment options, which allows businesses to launch applications quickly without the need for complex infrastructure management. These platforms also provide tools for monitoring and managing applications after deployment, enabling businesses to track performance, fix bugs, and make updates as needed. The ease of deployment is one of the reasons why low-code and no-code platforms are so appealing to businesses, as they reduce the time and cost involved in getting applications up and running.

The impact of low-code and no-code platforms on building enterprise solutions cannot be overstated. These platforms enable businesses to develop applications faster, reduce development costs, and empower non-technical users to participate in the development process. As these platforms evolve and offer more advanced capabilities, they will continue to play a key role in helping organizations address complex business challenges and drive digital transformation. With the ability to integrate with existing systems, scale to meet growing demands, and ensure security and compliance, low-code and no-code platforms are becoming essential tools for enterprises looking to innovate and stay competitive in the digital age. By leveraging the power of these platforms, businesses can create custom solutions that are tailored to their unique needs, ultimately enhancing efficiency, productivity, and overall business performance.

www.ingramcontent.com/pod-product-compliance
Lightning Source LLC
LaVergne TN
LVHW051231050326
832903LV00028B/2338